Ch

*"The race is not given to the swift, but those who endure to the end".*

*~Ecclesiastes 9:11 KJV*

On Friday, February 26th, 1993 I was brought into the world by two young teen parents. There were stories told at family gatherings how of much my parents were so in love with each other at the time. My dad had been the star football player at Columbus Senior High, and my mom was a student at Homestead Senior high, playing basketball as an extracurricular activity. My mother parents are African-American and my dad parents are Bahamian and African-American. Teen parenting back then was not as popular as it is now in our generation, which is why those same children left their mothers to raise their child. Due to that I lived with my grandmother while my mom started college and still living life as a young adult. I attended Rainbow Christian Academy at the very tender age of 3. We had a routine every morning. The teacher first said a

1

prayer and then the class would recite the pledge of allegiance. We studied stories in the bible. The students were also graded on versus in the bible based on how well we could recite them.

My first-grade teacher was named Ms. Glass and she made sure I stayed on top of my work. I always scored high in every subject. When I was in the second grade, I entered a spelling bee. I was very shy and nervous but surprisingly, I was one of the finalist. Third grade was my last year attending private school, at the award ceremony I received a certificate for best math student and best smile of the year. During this stage in my life I was very insecure because of my weight as a little kid, I was heavier than most kids. This made it difficult for me to feel comfortable to stand up in front of a group of people. Every day, I had a routine. My grandmother Denise, who I lived with, worked very early in the morning. My aunt Cruella and I had to take her to work six days out of the week and then drive back home so she could get her and I ready for school. She would take me to my grandmother's sister, Aunt

Doris house, which was not too far from our house. During that time, she was attending Hills Borough Senior High School. Once we were up and ready to take my grandma to work, I stayed awake until it was time to get ready for school. I loved to watch the Barney show as a little girl. I repeatedly asked my aunt to rewind the video every time it went off. Surely it made her upset most mornings, if not every morning with my whining because she was just a teenager. But my mom was living her life and kept getting in all kinds of trouble so most times Aunt Cruella was left to care for me. My uncle Willie drop me to school and my two smaller cousins off to school and pick us up every day. Those days were clear to me. He drove a light blue van and he was so upset and aggravated at the fact that I was always forgetting something at the house, like my lunch box. One day I went to school with my hair wild because no one remembered to do it. My grandmother was at work and aunt Cruella was most likely rushing to get to school. My uncle reminded me that my hair wasn't done and said, "I don't do girls hair" and we walked out the door. My 1st grade teacher noticed that my hair was wild and we were going on a field trip to sing Christmas carols. She was glad to fix my hair for the performance. She took a rubber band to do my hair and a ribbon from the Christmas reef on the classroom door to make a bow. I remember buying pizza every Thursday, and Friday had become ice cream day.  One year, I didn't have money for pizza and my dad brought me a whole box of pizza to the school. I was so embarrassed. I was overweight and for him to bring me the big pizza box to have alone made me feel very uncomfortable in front of my peers. Of course, I shared with the class, but the fact that he bought a whole entire pizza was embarrassing to an overweight third grader. Today, I can laugh about it but back then I was truly embarrassed.

My dad and I spent plenty of time together when I was a little a girl. My younger sister from another mother was also along for the ride. I remember riding down South Beach as he hollered at the women walking the strip. From what I can recall he always had the women surrounding him and a different woman every visit. There was, maybe one or two faces that was familiar but all others he had in rotation. He loved Hooters and whenever I would visit his house, that was our dinner. He lived in a 3-story home in the Grove. The first floor had slot machine and the second floor was the entertainment room/living room. My dad bought my very first Nintendo game boy. I remember having that game boy specifically because it had a camera in the back and everyone was surprised that I had one. Everyone else had games but thought mine was cooler. There was also gave me a printer that allowed me to print out pictures. Every day after school, I immediately hopped on the computer after completing my house chores and homework. In those times, it was not much social media but there were chat rooms. When my cousins would come over for the weekend we would play all day on my computer and most likely doing things we weren't supposed to at that age. As I got older I then stopped using the computer as much, unless there was work to be done. We then converted from young children in to our mid-teens where we became interested in chat lines and cell phones instead of

Barbie dolls. We were living in a generation that was rapidly evolving.

I was removed from private school because my dad stopped giving my mother money for my tuition and it became too hard for her and my grandmothers to pay alone. My mother found ways to try and keep me in the private school and as well as keeping me well dressed. Those ways resulted in what we call today, "hustling". She finally decided to try to put a stop to all the wrong doings, pulled me out the private school and placed me into public school and was on the job hunt. I noticed it had become very difficult for her to find a great paying job because of her back ground, but I knew one day, God would make a way. As a result, my mom not being able to find or keep a job, she would go back to her wrong doings. My grandmother was left to care for me while my mom was still growing as a young adult. There were plenty of days that I would go without seeing my mom because she was out trying to make a living. She stole items from different designer stores and made thousands of dollars in profit when she sold the merchandise to the streets to keep me dressed and money in her pocket. She wanted to keep up with the life style of me being a child of well-known football player. Whenever I would go to visit my grandmother Doris-Ann, my great grand-mother Albertha, and my aunt Ruby, they would ask where my mom was and I was told to say I didn't know or she was out of town but knowing she was really in jail. So, when things like this happened it was the norm to say she was out of town.

My mother lived with a guy she was dating at a time, but I insisted on living with my grandmother Denise because I had become so attached to her. He was very nice to me but I cling on to my grandmother. This lead to my aunt Cruella also having to be the main care giver when my grandmother was at work. I sensed her frustration of living with a toddler who was not hers, that was spoiled and always wanted to rewind Barney VHS tapes. During her teenage years I was the snitch. I remember telling my grandmother Denise that she went and got a tongue ring in her mouth and my grandmother took her

back to the tattoo shop for them to take it out. Still until this

day she always reminds me of that. Like my mother, my

grandmother was a single mom. She was not receiving

consistent help from my mothers' father. You see, this epidemic

too often takes place in African-American homes. Everyone

thought that one day I would be a statistic; another un-wed or

uneducated teen.  My mom from my understanding was not a

very easy child to raise. She always stayed in trouble, was

always fighting, and in her young adult years always going to

jail. Although my mom went on to a HBCU in Miami to continue

her studies after high school, she didn't finish. My maternal

grandmother told me of a story of when my mom told her at 16

she would get a boyfriend and at 17 she was going to have a

baby, and here I am today. My paternal grandmother of course

did not like the idea of my dad impregnating my mother being

that they were so young and it was the beginning of my dad's

football career. As a young child, I was always involved in

church. I was first a member of St. John Missionary Baptist

Church in Naranja, Fl. I lived near the homestead air force base in Homestead, Fl. Church was about a 4/5-minute drive from our home. Every Sunday my grandmother would send me to church whether she was there or not. I sung in the youth choir along with my older cousin who is like a sister to me. Also, I danced with a church and family friend all the way up unto the age of 9. Sundays were the best.

I loved coming home from church smelling my grandmother Denise fresh greens, fried chicken, and homemade sweet potato pie. There was obviously more on the menu on Sundays, but those smells just set in. Everyone in our family, including the pastor's family from church, would come over to eat and she never mind. She made all the food stretch and everyone had the opportunity to eat a nice hot Sunday meal. I eventually stopped attending the church after the mix up of pastors and I started lingering more around my Paternal grandmother Doris-Ann Warren Ferguson and our family's church. There, I grew up in a small family oriented church. It was a small white church with bricks in Coconut Grove, Florida.

There was never a big congregation, mostly just our family who owned the church. My great grandfather is the founder and built the church from the ground up. He was a Bahamian from the island of Sung Corner Acklins in the Bahamas. For years, he was the leader and pastor until he the Lord decide to call him home in 1994. He accepted Jesus Christ as his personal savior at a very early age and attended seminary in Nashville, Tennessee where he studied Theology. He began ministering at St. Paul Baptist Church, Nassau Bahamas under another pastor. He was ordained a minister in 1945. He served in the capacity as Associate Minister at Mt. Olive Missionary Baptist Church in Ft. Lauderdale, Fl. Spreading the gospel continuously, he ministered in a little wooden building better known as Mess Hall to all the labor camp workers of the Redlands. Rev. Theodore Gibson in the early 1950's along with the late Rev. Ferguson led a civil rights movement march, to integrate Metro-transit, McCory's and Virginia Beach. He was instrumental in causing integration within Dade county school system beginning with Vineland Elementary, Palmetto Junior and Senior schools. He was a very hard worker, and a faithful servant of God. A contractor by trade, he also served as secretary to the ministers and deacons union. He was a member of the Masonic Family union. He has made an impact of the lives of his family, church, and community. I was only 1 when he passed back in 1994. My older cousins always told me stories about when he passed. Being a toddler not understanding or knowing what was going on, I was asking for a bowl of grits that morning. We all gathered at his and my great-grandmother home singing and praying as he transitioned into heaven.

My great grandmother Albertha Ferguson, his wife, also known as Granny, was the First lady of course and she still lives until this day at the age of 90 plus years old. This distinguished matriarch and loving neighbor would feed anyone whether they had money or not. She is very devoted to God, her family, and her community. She understands that every deed performed is an opportunity to serve God by serving his people.  As a little girl, I always wanted to go over to spend time with Granny. She enjoys swimming in the pool to exercise her legs as the doctor sometimes instructed her. Most kids couldn't talk about fun things that they do with their great grandmothers, so I felt extra blessed to had been able to hang out with her. We loved to eat so anything we did involve food.  Every Wednesday and Sunday I was dropped off to her house for Bible study and church and whenever there was dance practice she and her live-in daughter carried me.

# Chapter 2

*"Let the little children come to me, and do not hinder them, for the kingdom of heaven belongs to them."*

*~Matt. 19:14 NIV*

Church was the most exciting activity to me as a young child. I enjoyed going because my dad side of the family were always doing family activities that allowed me to bond with my cousins who were my age. I had one cousin who's house I loved to spend the night at every chance I had and she was so excited for me to come being she was the only child. Like any other cousins, we fussed and disagreed a lot but we always ended back at square one defending one another. This cousin grew up a little bit more spoiled than I ever was, so sometimes she had an issue with the truth and we always ended up getting into childish arguments.

I started Junior high school at Campbell Drive Middle. I remember spending the night in Fl. City at my great-grandmother Pearlie Curry, also known as" Mommae" house to be able to catch the bus to school. She lived right across the street from Florida City park. I really disliked going down there because she never had the AC on and besides the fact that I loved staying in my own home. Mommae grew up in a small town in Lamont, Florida. Every time I went to her house as a kid if my cousins and I misbehaved, she would give us good old fashion whooping. She made us pick out a switch of the tree that planked in the front of the house. Although she spanked us she would never let our parents discipline us when she was around. Whenever one of the children didn't agree with any of the adults we all ran to Mommae. She always sent us to the grocery store down the street from the house whether it was to get that bacon that you could barely chew or snacks to keep us full and calm. She always called me a sweet little girl and to let her know if my mother ever bothered me.

Eventually at the very beginning of 7th grade I auditioned at Author Polly and Mays Middle school for the chorus magnet program because my mother thought I should attend a better school, and I was accepted, so, I transferred. This time I could stay home and catch the bus from where I lived with about a 5 min walk to the bus stop. Out of all the years of schooling, that was my very first time of riding the school bus to and from school every day. This made it up to me if I got to school on time versus always being late, if my mom or someone else in my family had to drop me off.

My grandmother Denise stayed working early shifts and often she was not able to take me to school. Most times, my mom would take me when she wasn't working. But the dilemma came about when she would either not be home to take me or late taking me. Middle school days were some of the best days of my life. I've always been very friendly so I was excited to meet new friends. The experience of learning different techniques and styles of singing was phenomenal. I had a very close male friend who was mean with the baritone voice. His voice went deeper than any ocean and could go high as any mountain when he wanted to. We learned to read music of course, we were graded by it. We also learned keyboard because that was a part of our class. I never really enjoyed keyboard more than my close friend did. He was more hands on with the keyboard and could play by ear. Playing by ear in the life of keyboard and theory is to be able to hear a sound and play it back. Not only did we learn to read music and play keyboard, we learned the different history of music and we mainly listened to Mozart and Beethoven. We were quizzed on listening to different orchestras play on a CD and we would have to guess the composer, year and name of the piece being played. As 8th graders we were reading music on high school and college level. I competed at Coral Reef Senior High for a chorus event, our solo along with two others rated superior. Our class received an excellent rating. Our instructor at that time reminded us that we were advance than most and by the time we got to college we would know how to read music and he was correct. Although, my skills today aren't as great as I would like, with a little more practice and time, I'm sure to have it down pack. My very first real boyfriend was in the 7th grade.

Edward was my very first love. I met him when I first transferred to Mays middle from Campbell Drive middle. He was 6'2 light skinned with long legs and loved the game of basketball. His favorite player was Kobe Bryant. Kobe was his idol and he often visited New Jersey in the summer to visit his mom because he lived with his dad and stepmom in Miami. I was so excited about this boyfriend that I could tell my mom about him and he was able to come to my 13th birthday jam. He was 14 years old going into high school and I was getting ready to go into the 8th grade. Head over heels for this guy I felt he could do no wrong. We even talked about the future and if we would end up married. Everything seemed perfect. Then we were having problems from back when Myspace was a popular social network, with girls writing on his page and me suspecting him to have conversed with them. I had a best-friend named Brianna from my younger childhood days who of course knew everything about me. When my cell phone was out of service I would call and text him from her phone. Until one day I was out of town with my cousins from my dad side and I ran into some other young boys.

They were there with their family and my cousins and I were visiting Orlando with our family. We exchanged numbers and all linked up at the pool area. There was this one guy who liked me and had gotten real close to me. Close to me in ways you wouldn't imagine even as someone to be their first day meeting them. Later down the week I returned from vacation and couldn't wait to tell her all what happened in Orlando, the guy that I met, and everything we'd done. Edward who was my boyfriend at the time, was acting as if he didn't want to be in the relationship anymore and I caught him talking to a girl long before the trip to Orlando. Expressing my time and experience resulted in her going back to tell him and him breaking up with me. The craziest part about this story is how he broke up with me. Or "they" rather. My now ex-best-friend Brianna, was moved to #8 to #1 on his top friends from Myspace, then there was a comment saying; "I love you baby". This instantly triggered in me to ask him if they were now a couple and he told me yes with no hesitation. I eventually called her once I pieced everything together. I asked her if she told Edward what we discussed on the phone about the trip, not really telling me yes or no, but I know that I was highly upset and ready to fight at that point. This was extremely hurtful that someone I called my best friend from the age of 3 years old would do something like that to me. We spent the night at each other's house, spent most summers together, and whatever I had she had and there was no in- between.

My grandmother and mom always told me it will always be the ones that are closest to you that want what you have or jealous of what you have, even if you don't have much. I was not very focused in middle in school I had so much going on at home so trying to keep up and adjust to a new school with new people was difficult.

Graduation from middle school was coming up, so I had to start to think of the high schools I wanted to attend. I never really had a preference on which school I would attend because I never really had a choice, it was always up to my parents. Of course, they didn't want me to go to just any school. I applied for two of the best high schools in South-Dade, Miami but did not get accepted because my grades weren't so well. My final option was Miami Southridge Senior High. One of the reasons for choosing this school is because I would have a way to and from, because my cousin, whose one year older than me, attended the same school so that I would have dependable transportation.

Nervous and shaken up I entered high school with the fear of who I would hang with and who would like me as person. I was still getting use to attending schools with wild children and students who interrupted the teacher every chance they were given. My first day of high school I was late, I knew some people but no one at the same time. I was never really that girl in school who was popular and had a lot of friends. Most of my friends were family and a few were older. I met two of the very best-friends anyone could ever ask for in 9th grade. Although both were older, only one of them were in a grade higher than us. She had been someone that I met through my ex-boyfriend Edward from middle school. It is very amusing how we met. Edward was close friends with her boyfriend at the time.  He told them that I was mean to him, I made him walk from the high school to the middle school to see me, and he also told them I took all his money. As if he had a lot for me to want to spend in the first place. My best friend Dayna thought because of what he told her and her boyfriend at the time that, that was the type of girl I was so at first, she was not really into me. I never knew the whole time that I had been dating a compulsive liar. He made it seem as if I was chasing him and he wasn't chasing me. I wasn't into having a boyfriend at the time because I was not really allowed to and I was involved in so many things at church I didn't have the time.

It was through my cousin Tara that I met my next boyfriend Jose. During this time, we met at Tara's boyfriend's, graduation party. They were older than us and we had just reached high school; Tara was beginning her sophomore year, and I was just a freshman. Jose caught me by selling dreams and feeding lies in my ear. He was talking about his job, all the career goals he had, and what he planned his future to be. Jose always had to be the center of attention and showed out everywhere he went on top of the fact that he couldn't really dress. Well, he was not what I was used to. Eventually I realized that I was only talking to him because my cousin Tara boyfriend was his best friend and I was always there with her, north of where I lived on the weekends. I distanced myself from him and he was not ready to let me go but he did. Sometimes I think he still holds that grudge against me but I was only 15-16 and it was clear that I wanted more out of life than he did back then.

I met my high school sweetheart Stanley and the rest was history. We met at a Quince for one of our friends from school. His friend CJ wanted to talk to me first but I did not like his cocky attitude, from that moment on Stanley approached me and it was him and I since that day. 2009-2010 I joined the cheerleading squad because I wanted to be that cheerleader girlfriend with the boyfriend that plays football but most importantly I needed an activity to do after school instead of just going home. When I first decided to try out for the squad I thought about all the things that would come along with it. Like the drama. My relationship with Stanley started off wrong. He was dating a girl name Karen while trying to pursue me. Once we became friends and conversing on the regular I suspected she started getting suspicious. I never knew that he had a girlfriend or someone he was still dating until she sent me an upsetting message on Myspace. She came at me calling me names and sending threats that she was going to slice my throat. I called him and told him what she was saying to me and he told me that he wasn't in a relationship with her. The next morning, I went to school looking to talk to her about the message she wrote me. I searched for her all over the school for her that morning and I could not find her. Finally, I saw her near the end of the school day, when I approached her she had nothing to say and her friends all on a wall backing her up. Apparently, they were there to help her fight me over Stanley. Stanley had lied to us both but that did not give her any reason to say that she would slice my throat. Threats are not something that I take lightly so I remained on top of everything.

One of my cousins and I went to a party later that weekend and she was there. I told my cousin what happened in school earlier that week and she was still enraged so she wanted to fight her. I suggested that we leave it alone but she insisted so I followed. She asked every girl at the party who they were and if they were Karen but Karen didn't answer. Her friend stood in front of her and said; "please don't" that's when my cousin hit her and the fight broke out. At one point they were pulling each other's hair and Karen wouldn't let go of my cousin's hair so I jumped in and hit her a couple of times and finally she let her go. When I got back to school after the weekend I was called to the office about the fight. Karen and her mom were saying that they were getting a police report on me and I had to explain that she started with me first and messaged me on MYSPACE. For proof to defend my case, I printed out the messages so that I wouldn't get suspended from school. When Karen and her mom went to go file a police report, I filed one as well with the threats that she sent me. Those threats would cause her to be kicked out of the school if I felt threatened for my life but I still had a heart so I didn't proceed with the report. It just caused me not to be suspended from school. Yes, after all of this I still stayed with Stanley because he had done nothing to me. Our relationship felt so real and I was very happy with him. My mom had just started letting me date when I started dating Stanley. His mom was such a sweetheart but his dad didn't come off so friendly, but I didn't take it to heart because that is how some people are and they may not mean any harm. The sister who lived in the home, seemed nice but her moods with me were up and down, and we never really held a conversation. In high school we had so many arguments because he was rude. Stanley never thought about how somethings he did affected our relationship but it didn't make me love him any less. Once there was a girl who was trying to talk to him on more than a friend level. Always, I wondered why this certain female was repetitively staring at me with a slight mean mug on her face. He then came to me to tell me that she tried to push up on him. So, the next time she gave me that look I was enraged. My cousin Anthony who played football as well told me to chill so I did and thought about what I had to lose by fighting her at school. Moreover, we were sitting for lunch and someone went over to ask her what was the problem she said she didn't have one, but there had to be a reason she was looking at me in a very disrespectful manner for me not to have known her. Additionally, that lead to me fighting her closest friend in school because she was feeding off of her negative energy. I was suspended for all of 3 days and was able to return back to school based off the fact that I had never been in any trouble. I had never gotten into a fight before so for me to have had one, someone had to mess with me first. Overall, I'm a very friendly person. I come off too friendly sometimes but I had to learn to observe people first. Before I started my very first semester in college, Stanley and I had a long talk about what we would do as far as the relationship was concerned. I suggested that we become friends so I can prevent myself a broken heart if he was to cheat but he insist that we could make the relationship work.

I told him about the talk I had with my older cousin Shardea who is like sister to me and that she was giving me advice on how I should always guard my heart. Stanley was in college playing football and I knew what came with players being that I saw my dad go through it firsthand. I didn't want to take the risk of dealing with heartbreak so I suggested we just end the relationship so he wouldn't feel as if I was taking his college experience from him. He figured that if his sister and her boyfriend could do it, we could too. He was so upset that I mentioned even breaking up, but I was truly only trying to protect my heart. I love very hard and I will do anything for the person I love, and if I was to find out he cheated on me while I was being loyal it would have truly torn me apart.

# Chapter 3

*"Thou shall not eat from the tree of knowledge of good and evil"*

*~Genesis 2:17 NIV*

……. But I ate the fruit, and my eyes were opened.

When I first went to college and moved to Tallahassee I was assigned to roommate with a girl from Gainesville, Florida named Paisley. I wrote her on Facebook introducing myself and letting her know I was going to be her roommate but I didn't get any response. After orientation, I arrived to the dorms to get my key to start moving my stuff in the apartment style dorm. I was also with a friend from high school named Roxanne who was also attending the same college. Once I finished moving all my things in the dorm, I was so frustrated because I was not use to sharing a room with anyone. Since Paisley didn't message me back on Facebook I thought that she wasn't coming or that she wasn't a very nice person so I switched her name on the door with another girl who was in our dorm name Maria. Maria was

Puerto Rican from Jacksonville, Florida and was very nice when I first met her. The dorm director came in and noticed that the names were changed and insisted that we change them back. I was embarrassed that Paisley had to find out that I switched her name that I didn't know what to do. My mother invited her to the family dollar with us to go get a few more things that I needed and told her to get a couple of things as well. Paisley, like me, lived and partially raised by her grandmother. Growing up wasn't easy for her at all. Both parents were drug addicts and her grandmother that took her in after her older sister moved, was an alcoholic. I knew God placed her in my life for a reason.

Samantha, another friend from high school, was expected to come to school in Fall and live in an apartment with me and Paisley. We all signed the lease together to live in the same apartment when she came. Samantha and I had become very close in high school our 11th grade year when I made the cheerleading squad. We seemed to have so much in common at the time as far as career goals and what we wanted to do after high school was a big concern. In high school had a virtual class together and used most of our class time planning things for college. At the time she was the only friend I had who was talking about going away to college. We would hang outside of school and her parents always let us use their cars to go out to the teen events. I started spending almost every weekend with her when I was not with my cousin on the north side of Miami.

Like everyone I imagined that we would be perfect roommates but it did not work out that way. Samantha did not like to clean. I knew of this from when we were in high school but figured college would change her, especially because she was sharing a bathroom with another female. Paisley and I were the main 2 of the 4 roommates that thoroughly cleaned. Our 4th roommate was never there so she barely needed to clean but when she was there she cleaned as well. There was a time when I cleaned the bathroom so well. I mean down on my knees and everything, and she went in there while her feet were dirty from

her sandals she had worn that day and did not wipe out the tub.
I was so upset with her that I took the very expensive bathroom
set out of the bathroom since she did not want to clean. The
reason for that was because I texted her and asked her to clean
it and she gave me a very rude response. I was pissed because I
always cleaned the bathroom with no problem at all.

Additionally, October of 2011 my great- grandmother
had a 90th birthday party. I was rushing out the house and left
an egg pot in the kitchen sink. My grandmother party was in
Miami and I was gone for 3 days. When I came back the same
pot was still in the sink and the entire house stunk because
Samantha did not clean. Even though when I cleaned the
kitchen before I left, that was the only thing that was left. From
that moment on we were never on good terms, mostly because
of the things she would let come out of her mouth to say to me
and things she would say to other people. Samantha made it
seem to others that we were being rude and nasty when in fact
it was her that was. She was also planning to move in with her

boyfriend once he graduated high school. We did not want to live with her anymore and signed a lease elsewhere for the following year. Roxanne and Flo are two girls who were best friends that I became close with my senior year of high school. They also were attending the same college.

It was summer of 2011 and his name was Isaiah. It was my older cousin Shardea birthday, and he was there along with one of her closest friend brother who is like family to us. The next day I had instant messaged on Facebook stating that he wanted to get to know me a little better. This was the funniest thing ever because I almost never respond to people on Facebook asking me out. I was angry at Stanley about a picture with him in a sandwich of females my cousin Ruby sent to me from the club so I figured it was ok for me to go out with this guy. The first thing he asked was, "are you going out to the club 20/20?". As a freshman, I would say I wasn't as wild as the others that had just jumped off the porch. Before college I was coached long before I attended to know the ins and outs and dos and don'ts'. I am extremely blessed to have had older family members who had gone through the whole college ordeal to show me how to get through. I explained to him that I did not come to college to spend my money on the club and the only way I was going was if he brought me the money to go and he did. From the time he brought me the money we started talking almost every day. After spending time at the club, he picked me up from the dorm I was living at, then we went to his house for a night of Friday and chill. At first, I was very nervous and scared. I had my roommate Paisley to write down his full name and address before I went anywhere with him. This was my first time ever meeting a guy and going off somewhere with him. Friday and chill turned out to being one of the most eventful nights of my life. When we first arrived at his home, it was very dark and I could not see. Because it was dark I'm assuming he had the master bedroom which was upstairs. We watched the movie until he began to start feeling on me. Going there I never had the intention on having sex with Isaiah. It was one of those things that kind of happened. He began to wrap his long strong tatted arms around me. Although my first was my high school sweetheart Stanley, I had never been touched the way he touched me. My heart started trembling, my legs started shaking and my whole body felt numb. Sex meaning had gone from just being ok to the best thing that had happened to me. After we finished what it felt like making love for the first time, on the first night, I was never the same.

Suddenly, I started to feel guilty about having sex with him because I was still dealing with Stanley. I was even supposed to spend the night that night but I was ready to go. I almost cried in the car telling Isaiah that I had to tell Stanley what happened, of course he told me not to, but I felt like I needed to. The next day he texted me and said that he never wanted to hurt me or for me to feel like he had taken advantage of me but I told him not to worry because it was something that I thought I wanted as well. I just didn't know what this meant for me and Stanley. From then on, I finally came out of my feelings and into my senses that my ex would not tell me anything about his other females, or let alone what he had going on period, so I did not feel the need to open my mouth. I know that you are probably thinking tit for tat isn't good, but being naïve at the time was not either. Stanley older sister Yolanda was very friendly. Once I saw the picture of him with the girls. I called her to vent to her about how it made me feel. She said that she didn't know what had gotten into him because their parents didn't raise them that way. She also expressed to me her love for Stanley and that his nephews, her children, looked up to him.  So, for him to carry himself in that manner was very distasteful. I continued to deal with Isaiah because Stanley did not care that he had hurt me and Isiah filled all my fantasies and more. He called and we spent time together whenever we were not in school. When I was with him I felt safe and secure. No one could hold me the way he held me. He was out every weekend and I knew that he was entertaining other females but it never bothered me. We never rushed for a relationship because I was still kind of in one with Stanley even though he never called. Isaiah was messing around with numerous of females that I knew nothing of. He was the kind of guy that was always hanging out in the clubs and the females would come to his section in the club to talk to the whole crew. I was the girl who was always in the house learning to cook. I was not perfect and still not but I was a little more tamed than most and I believe that is what made Isaiah like me the most. For months, we were dealing with each other heavy enough to build a very strong friendship/bond. When we caught ourselves catching feelings we would both back up because obviously we knew each other's situation. There were plenty of nights he would come over and I was just learning how to cook, he would try my food even if it wasn't good, and that meant something to me on top of it being hilarious. His friends would come over with bottles to play games with my roommates and friends. We all had plenty of fun nights.

Sex was at a very high demand when it came to him and I. There were plenty of times I would become sick and thinking that I was pregnant because of how much we were sexually active. I started vomiting everywhere. I could not figure what was wrong with me. I ended up making an appointment with a gynecologist in Miami. The doctor examined me and told me that I was not pregnant but I had developed a sexually transmitted infection that could be solved in the matter of days with the medication he was going to provide. About a month or two after I found this out, I was also developing symptoms of Lupus and wasn't aware what was going on with my body.

This made it easier for me to contract the infection. Stanley, my ex-boyfriend was the one that took me to the emergency room. I had been telling him that I was feeling sick from a couple of months at this point and he thought that it was me being lazy and complaining. I had been feeling fatigue and nauseous on top of the fact that I was losing a tremendous amount of weight. At the time when the doctor brought my results back in the room they still didn't detect that I had a chronic illness. They only that I had contracted an infection which caused swelling to my lymph nodes.

When Stanley came back in the room I told him what happened, I told him about Isaiah and all the things we did and that I had unprotected sex with him. He stepped outside I believe to calm down and make a phone call. Eventually, he came back in sat down and once I was discharged he took me home. There was complete silence on the ride home besides me asking him what we were going to do as a couple at this point. He kept saying that he didn't know; I was heartbroken, and scared all at the same time. I was thinking that this was the worst thing I could have ever done to someone that I truly loved even if it was to get back at him. Stanley finally broke down and told me that he had been messing around and had sex with 12-13 different females and did what the generation calls today "run a train" on a female with a close roommate Robinson. This information really hurt me but I really had no place at that point to speak on it.

All I knew what that we both really messed up. We decided that we would stick through this obstacle in our relationship and move on to better things. For months everything was going well but I was still feeling sick and losing more weight. My grandmother Doris-Ann had just been told that she didn't have many months to live and I was still dealing with Stanley. She passed in November.

# Chapter 4

***"For I am now ready to be offered and the time of my departure is at hand. I have fought a good fight, I have finished my course, I have kept the faith"***

***~II Timothy 4: 6-7 KJV***

November 30, 2012 is the last breath my paternal grandmother took. While with the city of Miami Police Department, she met my loving grandfather, Michael Warren and they married February 14, 1991. My grandpa preceded in death after 21 years of marriage in December of 2010. My grandmother vibrancy, zest, and enthusiasm for life were evident. Her living testament has always been her love and loyalty to her family, church and community. She always tried to help someone along the way. I spent every summer with her and Grandpa Mike, along with 3 of my cousins. Every year she would make us do work around the house whether it was folding clothes or picking up sticks after the small summer storms that use to take place.

Then take us to Nashville to enjoy the amusement park called Dollywood. Although she only lived 2 hours from Nashville we always got 2 rooms and stayed for at least two days. I remember going to the Bahamas spring break when I danced at the church with my cousins. I went with money but she always took care of me. My grandma was the life of the party. She was all about fun and love. One year, we went on a family vacation to her house and she started throwing dollar bills over the balcony from her room to the living room floor. Everyone went wild trying to pick up the one and five dollar bills off the floor. My dad had plenty of football games when I was little and she was there to carry me to every single one. The times we shared are unforgettable and if I explain, it will probably turn into another book. When she left me, for the first time in my life I knew exactly what it meant to become speechless. I was worried about the rest of my years in college because her and the grandmother I lived with were the main people putting me through. When the doctors had given her word on the last days she could live, she wanted to have a talk with my grandmother

Denise to discuss me. At the time, I was 19 years old and a freshman in college. She told my grandmother Denise that she was not going to be around long and for her not to worry about me because I will be taken care of. My grandmother Denise said to me that when she was there grandma Doris couldn't really get a chance to talk to her and she was hesitant about some of things she was saying because my aunt was around. My aunt, who was my grandmother Doris baby sister, then began to tell her that she was getting ready to leave to go to the store insinuating that my grandma Denise needed to leave. My grandma Denise said she nodded her head in agreeance with her not to worry about me.

*Daughter. Spend your life loving. Not seeking love. Ocean need not seek water.*

*~Jaiya John*

I knew of myself very well and who I dealt with as far as sex was concerned. The first person I called was not my ex Stanley because I had not seen or touched him for months during the time I was involved with Isaiah. I called Isaiah to ask him who else he was having unprotected sex with because he knew the type of female I carried myself to be and I just could not believe that he would think about being that irresponsible. Going insane on the phone with him he told me about one girl and then apologized very sincerely for it but from then on, I lost all contact with him and kept moving on with my life as I was taught. Months later I found out that he had a child on the way. This information made me call him instantly because he had just told me he was not involved with anyone when our situation happened. Before I found this out I had a friend who told me about the girl he was involved with heavily. She started to explain how she was talking to other dudes and carrying herself in a nasty, non-lady like manner. She also said how the girl knew she was pregnant but it was not by Isaiah, it was from another guy. The other guy told her to have an abortion because he did not want to have a baby with her, so I figured she tried put the baby on him. After I called Isaiah and warned him that I knew about him and his new baby mother I also told him to be careful and to make sure he gets an DNA test. Months later after the baby was born he contacted me on the social network,

Instagram. He commented on a picture I posted that stated;

*"When you have a relationship with God everything works out in*

*your favor"* and he said, true. I responded with a smart remark

and he told me to call him. That day I texted him and asked him

what was up? He replied to me and said; "I don't have a jit". As I

read the message I didn't know if I should be smiling full of

happiness or enraged that he thought to tell me he didn't have

a child. From my understanding he found out that the baby

wasn't his at the hospital so I know it messed him up. That point

on we would talk every day. I noticed he still was doing that

late-night thing but it didn't matter as long as he was texting

me.

One week after my birthday It was spring break of 2013

and I was finally able to enjoy it in Miami as a 21-year-old. I

always planned to celebrate my birthday during spring break

because the week of my birthday was usually midterms.

Moreover, this was a time expected to be great, my little sister was even able to join me when I came down as well. Never forgetting this day, I was with a couple of other family and friends. On the way I got into a car accident with a lady who barely spoke English, so when it was time to call the cops no one knew what the driver wanted to say or do. Once the cops were called we established that it was no damage on either car and we exchanged information and went about our way. I was in town freaking out not only because I got in the accident but because we were on our way to the beach with alcohol in the car.

When we arrived at the beach we parked in the parking garage on 7th ave and start walking up to Ocean Dr. Anthony was one of the other family members that met us at South beach, he had just come down from school, along with our friend/classmate Brandon. Whenever I was around those two I felt at home and comfortable without any weird feeling or vibe. After being out on the beach all day and dropping everyone off, I finally got home and settled down. The following Sunday before leaving to go back Tallahassee for school, I found myself

vomiting and by this time I was weighing 135 pounds and not

able to eat as much. My mother demanded that I go to the

hospital before leaving to go back to school.

Finally, after so many hours of the wait, a doctor came in and

examined me. I had given him all the symptoms that I had been

feeling for the past couple of months. He then ordered the

nurses to run different test on me and we waited for the results.

Once he saw the lesions that began to develop on my elbows

from this hidden disease, he instantly said that he was admitting

me into the hospital. My results from the test ran showed that I

had high level of protein leakage in my urine which were putting

my kidney in danger, so he was sending a nephrologist to see

me the next morning along with a rheumatologist for the aches

and pains I had been experiencing.

# Chapter 5

*"See now that I, even I, am he, and there is no God beside me; I kill and I make alive; I wound and I heal; and there is none that can deliver out my hand"*

*~Deuteronomy 32:39 NIV*

March 21,2013 was the day I was diagnosed with Lupus Nephritis. I was the calmest when finding out because God had already prepared me for this. I put in my mind that I know going through this I would have some very bad days, but I would not let it get me down. I was put on all types of medication such as blood thinners, which were shots every day into my stomach to prevent blood clots the disease may cause. The steroid medication had me swelling up like a blowfish but it was something that I had to take to get better. I could barely fit in any of my clothes, I had to go buy new clothes. My family was all stirred up at the fact that I was diagnosed with this disease that apparently ran in my family, but I didn't find out until I was diagnosed. Of course, no one wanted to cry in front of me but they were so heartbroken by the fact that I had to live with a disease that has no cure.

I spent 2-3 weeks in the hospital ready to go home every day but I needed to be watched. My family brought me food daily to the hospital because I did not like the hospital food at all. My lupus was very active in my kidneys at this point I had to get a biopsy done. It took them forever to come take me but once I was in the room it took no longer than 45 mins and I had to lay flat on my stomach for 12 hours until the next day because they didn't want me bleeding anywhere else but where the kidney biopsy had been done. Once I was done with that I was able to go home a few days later. During this time Stanley and I were still having trust issues, I moved on from our situation but apparently, he didn't. When my grandmother passed and Stanley was not there to comfort me as I expected him to be. I could barely get him on the phone to talk. After being told that I have Lupus I immediately contacted him to let him know but of course he did not answer. It was not until I

contacted his sister Reesy to have her inform him, and

immediately he called right away. I was thinking at that moment

that he could not answer for me but he answered for his sister

and it made me feel as if he didn't love me as much as I loved

him. God was giving me a sign to let Stanley go right then, but I

didn't want to let go of the only thing I knew.

I was released March 27th and the next day was Stanley

birthday. Spring semester had just ended for him. I was so eager

to get out. I expressed to him that I wanted to take him to the

beach for lunch to celebrate his birthday the next day. I will

never forget he bought me a rose from a man who were selling

them down the strip. I felt so loved but I was so hot and tired

from being out the house in the heat. Even though I was not

permitted by the doctor to be out in that type off setting, I did

so he wouldn't feel bad for not doing anything with me for his

birthday. I loved spending time with Stanley because he made

me laugh and I was very comfortable around him. Once we

were home, we spent a little time together before him leaving to go home to get ready to head out with his friends at the club. My girlfriends felt some type of way that he was out at the club and I was home. They felt like he should have been there. I didn't want the whole world to revolve around me at the time so they didn't understand that it made me feel better he was out enjoying his 21st birthday. They also expressed that if someone loved me whole heartedly they would not care about a birthday that they could celebrate another time. At this point in my life I did not want to be left alone and although I had friends to talk to, when they are busy with their lives I had no one to talk to but God and Stanley at the time. Stanley, I noticed, never took anything I said serious and always thought of me as a whining complaining brat because he was under the impression that I was spoiled. I had to go back into the hospital that same night because of where I had been and it was too much fluid in my body. Stanley was nowhere to be found. I called him to let him know that I was going back to the hospital but for him to still go out and enjoy his birthday. Once I arrived at the hospital the next day I was told that I needed to have a blood transfusion and that it was urgent for me to get the blood transfusion that night. My parents were calling around telling family members what was about to happen.

Right before I was waiting to get the blood transfusion my dad walked in the door like he had been running to get there. My great aunt had given him the news that I was sick. I was not speaking to my dad during this time because I was still upset at the fact that he had not played a major part in watching me grow up and the fact that he did not attend my grandmother, his mother's own funeral. The last time I sat down to have a conversation with him was right before my senior year of high school when he picked up my little sister and I for us to reunite after so many years. There were stories of him not believing in God and walking the streets barefoot. Later, when the doctors were preparing the nurses to come in and give me the blood transfusion Stanley finally came through the door. It was almost midnight and he was getting ready to head back to school to finish off the spring semester. I was upset with him because I was calling him all day and texting him and I still did not get a response. He explained that he had just woke up from his night out and he was running errands for his mom, and he would be to the hospital once he finished but it ended up being late at night. Once he walked through the door my blood pressure instantly shot up. He barely said anything, and he was looking down at his phone for a long time. He suddenly chuckled and I asked what was funny, he told me "Nothing, my homeboy is sending a girl that likes me to pick me up from the airport tomorrow". I was thinking to myself why would he tell me something like that knowing we already have trust issues. I wanted to trust him but his actions kept showing me that I couldn't. To top it off, I was told the nurses had to postpone the blood transfusion because my blood pressure was through the roof.

Nevertheless, I asked Stanley to call me once he made it back to school, and of course he did not. I was always calling and texting Stanley to check on him, and other times I wanted

to vent. He never returned my calls and when he did it was days

later. There were times where I couldn't sleep and I would be

up all night waiting on him to call. I felt alone and that I had no

one on this earth. I had become so stressed about losing him it

brought about shingles along with type of the medication I was

taking at the time called Cellcept. At first, I thought I was just

getting a rash and began to scratch a little. After leaving a family

function, I took a look at my arm I saw tiny bumps going in on

direction on the left side. The next morning, I was beginning to

see the rash from on the left side of my chest around to my

back. The shingles was the worst experience of side effects from

Lupus I ever had. Most times the pain would be so unbearable

from the burning and itching, stay covered up from the sun and

I had to take oatmeal baths to sooth it. I tried all different kinds

of products to get rid of the shingles as fast as I could but

nothing seemed to work. The doctor explained to me that even

with the medication it will take a while to heal because I had

broken very bad. One night, I got down on my knees and prayed hard to ask God to remove him out of my heart and life so I would be able to focus on becoming healthy. God made me realize at that time that I did not need to depend on any man for joy and happiness except him. I took my focus off the Lord and thought that my life would be over if I was to lose Stanley.

Released from the hospital, and thanked God I never had to stay in the hospital more than 3 days since, now I am on medications and checking my blood pressure every day. I was worried about school and how I would be able to handle all the stress that comes along with being a college student and living with a chronic illness. I emailed all my professors the first time I was diagnosed to let them know my situation and knowing that I had a couple of weeks left before the semester was over. They all were understanding and I was allowed to make up work and turn in assignments via email, blackboard, etc. I remember stressing over school because I did not want to stop going and all the talk about me staying back home caused more stress.

When grades came out I was surprisingly shocked to know that had been my best semester yet. I was full of excitement and joy that I could do something so marvelous in such a hard time. It was then when I realized that I could not let anything stop me. My family and friends were more concerned with this illness than I was. My mind was already made up that I will not let this get me down because I don't believe that God will put you through situations and not bring you out of them.

There was lots of talk about me going back and whether or not my parents wanted me to stay away in school. I had to call around for doctors in Tallahassee to make sure that I was being seen on a regular basis. The nephrologist in Miami was concerned about me finding a great doctor that was going to take care of me like he did. He was very discrete about the things he said to me regarding changing doctors and adjusting to living with this illness. The insurance company I had was no good for my condition and it required me to pay out of the pocket a lot. I started applying for Medicaid and Disability since

I was not able to work or afford any insurance, especially as a college student. I spent in Miami the summer of 2013 dealing with my illness, and making appointments to see doctors. I was on so many different medications and my weight rose due to fluid from the medication. Once I found my doctors I was set and ready to go back to school in Tallahassee, Fl. August had come around and I finally came to realization that Stanley was not what I needed at that point in my life and that I was done with heartbreak so I moved on from Stanley. My older cousin had a party right before I left to go back and I remember listening to the song "lose to win" by Fantasia and anyone who knows me know that lyrics to a song means everything to me. I felt rejuvenated as a whole and instantly felt an urge to be free of heartache. He hurt me and I did not want to feel that hurt anymore. I texted him to let him know that I was done with all that he was putting me through and I was moving on to being single and learning how to love myself. Of course, he replied in a horrific outburst telling me that I didn't know what the fuck I wanted, and basically that I was oblivious to the things that was going on around me. I knew that I was a very smart girl when it came to knowing how I should and should not be treated.

Now that I was back in T-town I was refreshed and ready for a new start. With my health and healing my heart. I was able to sleep better, and not worry about Stanley. Hanging and getting out of the house was the groove I was getting back to. Before my epiphany, I was always in the house, crying and thinking about where he could be or what he could be doing. Stanley was so upset that I finally decided to be done with him he wrote a song bashing me. I wasn't concerned about how many people would hear it because Stanley music was not that popular. Like girls do, I was snooping around the internet and came across the song. He stated that I had an STD from someone but did not state it was an infection or all the things he had done. I was so upset I started crying immediately. I first called my mom and told her what happened and she told me not to worry about him. I wrote his sister Reesy and informed her of the song he made. I told her that he was giving out the wrong information and I was going to sue him, if he didn't remove it. Her message was very rude at first but then she came back and said that he was immature and that he will grow up, and she suggest I leave him alone. I told her that I already told him I was done and he kept on. After the message for whatever reason she unfriended me.

Although he didn't say my name particularly he did mention a girl he was in love with from high school. I told Isaiah about it. He explained to me that he was just mad and to ignore him because I knew the truth. Surprisingly he never bad-mouthed Stanley, he just reminded me that I deserved better. Even if I wasn't with him and that's what made me respect him more. Whenever I am in doubt about something I pray for an answer. Two months later I received a disturbing phone call. The call was from an old friend name Sharon who I grew up with in church that was dating one of Stanley close friends David. David was also like a brother to me even when Stanley and I were going through our times. Sharon informed me that she was going through David phone and she saw Stanley text telling David that he had gotten a girl pregnant. She didn't know if we were still together but she wanted to inform me. I was glad that she told me that because I was just beginning to feel like I had made a mistake. It had given me confirmation from what I already knew. He put someone else before me in the time where I needed him the most. He left. I started to blame myself for his wrong doings thinking it was get back from the situation with Isaiah. There couldn't have been so much hate in his heart for him to hurt me like that. When I found out, I was getting ready to head out for my school's homecoming weekend.

I decided that I would call him to let him know what I found out the next day after I was done having fun and I also called him to tell him what Sharon told me and he went off. He called David to let him know that Sharon had called me and he told him that she was doing it out of spite because she was mad at David and not genuinely looking out. Besides the fact that she was trying to get back at David she was also informing a childhood friend who she thought was still in a relationship with Stanley. Three months prior to this incident I visited him where he went to school in West Virginia. The day I was heading back home and Stanley was dropping me to the airport I found a condom in his car. During this time Stanley and I didn't use condoms so I know it was coming from wrong doings. His friend Mike was in the car. Mike lied for him and he told me that, that was his condom before Stanley could get a chance to answer me. Stanley forgot that he told me him and his dad were very particular about who drove his car unless he didn't want me driving it.

None of that mattered at that point I was livid. I got out the car and didn't say a word to him because at this point I was hurt and felt like I wasted money on going to see him. It is not until today that I realized God was trying to stop me from going to see him because I missed my departing flight going to see him and I had to buy another ticket. After I had gotten back from the trip I was starting to see Stanley and things differently.

I was ready to move in a new direction with my life and my heart.

Once I was back at school I found out that Isaiah had a seizure and was on a breathing machine, breathing only 10 % of oxygen with things not looking too good. It was that moment that I realized I truly cared about him. I was so heartbroken and in fear that I may lose someone that I could possibly have a future with because it was obvious Stanley and I were completely done. I stayed up praying every day and every night. I would send him text messages of scriptures from the bible to help him fight through even though I knew he couldn't read it. I went to revival every day for one week praying and fasting for the Lord to bring Isaiah through this. Calling his friend Tracy was no problem for me to get updates but Tracy couldn't give me that much information because he wasn't receiving that much himself. Weeks later I received a message from Isaiah's phone saying; "thanks for praying for me", and we started talking again from that point. I knew what the power of prayer can do but it was that text that made me a true believer. God showed me what he could do that day and that anything was possible. I was filled with all kinds of emotion when I received that text.

Shocked, surprised, and happy all at the same time to finally hear from him. We were both going through a storm in our lives at the same time. This made us converse more than usual and we were talking about this experience almost every day. I would talk to Isaiah about what happened with Stanley. As a friend first, he would give me male advice as to how I could not allow anyone to treat me less than I deserved. He felt as if Stanley was taking advantage of the person I was. It had become a routine that we spoke every morning and then all day until I went to bed then repeat. I noticed his change from being a party guy to wanting draw closer to God and calm down on all the wild things he was involved in. A wind of humbleness must have come over him and it started to show. Nevertheless, we had become so close we started developing stronger feelings I believe and he began to back away to prevent him from having those strong feelings for me. Guys are not always great at expressing themselves so I figured that was an excuse but I came to realization that we were close enough for him to tell me how he feels. One day he told me we were texting too much and we should slow down because stronger feelings were starting to develop. Although, I did not want the texting to end, I agreed to disagree because I was not going to talk to someone who thinks we were "talking too much" out of fear of committing to me. That day I felt unappreciated as friend because I wanted to be there through his transition after his traumatic event.

Two months after Isaiah and I stopped communicating, out of blue, Stanley texted me and asked if it was ok for him to meet up with me to talk. At first, I didn't want to because I wanted nothing to do with a person like that. He mentioned something about getting the girl pregnant and how he didn't want to continue with me because of what I had going on and he was "young". Enraged and full of disappointment I was lost for words at first. Once what he said registered in my mind and he went in the house I became even more angry. I sent him a text saying I was going to have my older cousin Jamil come to beat his ass. He didn't want to come out of the house. At this point I was ready to fight. I saw him peeking out the window to see if I left. I remember him telling me he was getting ready to leave so I parked on the side of the house waiting for him to pull out.

Once he did, I chased him up until I got caught by a red light. God showed up at the red light in that moment. I went ballistic and was thinking about all I had to lose by chasing this dead situation. As soon as I made a stop at the service station I called David. I broke down, I told him what happened and he stepped out the club to talk to me. He said he couldn't believe what Stanley had said to me and that I should leave him completely alone. I was crying angry tears and ready to literally kill Stanley. I surely wanted to be left alone after that and I never wanted to speak to him again. Stanley had shown his true colors and made it completely obvious that I was not what he wanted in his life.

Moving forward, I moved on from those two confusing situations. I was living life still as a single young woman. Several months went by and I was doing fine. I had a friend named Matt who was always there for me when I needed him. Matt and I met in college freshmen year in sociology class. We hung out with a group of friends and sometimes by ourselves. Matt was a preachers' kid so we connected on that level, although I'm a preachers' grandchild. One day I asked him to come over to get a frog that had come in my apartment while I was cleaning up. Matt always came over to hang and chill with me and Paisley. The next day after he got the frog out we hung out that night with drinks and playing games. We were in the kitchen on facetime with some friends and he kissed me. When he kissed me, I was in shock because we were only friends and I didn't see him in any other way besides the flirting he would do here and there. Once we talked about it, he then expressed that he had certain feelings for me and wanted to further them. I told him that I wasn't ready to be in a relationship being that I had just gotten over Stanley and trying to get over Isaiah who I grew to love. I finally gave into the idea. We began to talk more and we decided we would give our relationship a try with going further. Everything seemed fine. We went out on dates and was always together from that day forward. We both visited his hometown and I met his parents. They both were ministers of the word. I thought because they were ministers it gave a bonus for the developing relationship. However, I was completely wrong once things turned left. Matt had finally gotten a job a Walmart. He was excited to get it because he was tired of depending on his parents and side hustles to make money. When I met his mother she kind of had an idea that he was already doing wrong with his side hustle. She was correct. Nevertheless, he called one day and said that he had been let go of his job because he had gotten into a fight. He told me that a guy was being racist with him and they got into it.

One week later, while sitting in the living room of my friend house having girl talk per usual, my friend Lyrica asked if I knew that he got fired. When I asked her what happened, her story was different from the story he told me. She explained that Matt was asleep on the clock in his car while workers and supervisors had been calling him on the radio. He was instantly fired. She knew what really happened because she worked at the same Walmart. Before we started furthering our friendship I let him know that I didn't want to be hurt or lied to again. He knew what I had been through with Stanley. He assured me that he would never treat me that way but still he did. It was at that moment that I realized he had a problem with telling the truth. I never made Matt feel like he needed to have a money or a job to be with me, and I couldn't believe he would make up such a big tale. Furthermore, I ended things with him because I thought if he could lie about something small as that, what else could he come up with. I decided to stay away and move forward.

Nicole and I became very close friends at the time that she asked me to be the god mother of her daughter. She initially was assigned to be me my roommate when I moved to off campus apartments, but we ended up having Paisley upon request instead, who had finally signed her lease. I was so excited because I felt it was a privilege to be asked to be a godmother. I was in the child life from the time she was born up until her mother thought it was ok to get in between what Matt and use to have. The time when I found out he was lying about the job I was at her house. As a friend, she was upset that he would lie about something so small. Then, suddenly, she switched sides. She figured that I was being too mean to him but I was not about to start off our relationship with lies and I didn't want anyone like that around me. He then mentioned to her that I was upset that he asked me to sleep on an air mattress. Sometimes I may act bougie but I am not and I will never get upset about something like that. I just could not believe he would ask me that and I had a bed at home. I never made anyone feel bad because of what they didn't have because I didn't have it all. I am a firm believer that people should work hard to get where they need to be and you treat the janitor with the same respect as the CEO. Nicole answered the phone for him when he was calling to look for someone who he thought could talk me into taking him back. I told Nicole that I didn't appreciate the fact that she was even listening to anything he had to say because she didn't know him until I introduced the two. We got into an argument over the phone. I told her numerous of times that I didn't want to talk to him and she was insisting, but every time I said no. I stopped talking to Nicole because I felt like she didn't respect me or my decision not to deal with Matt. Our argument escalated into a physical altercation. It all began because my cousin was not up for her continuing to talk to him and not respecting how I felt about it. She wrote Nicole on twitter and told her she was going to beat her ass. I was upset that it had to get to that point and from that point our friendship went downhill. Nicole felt like I had been talking about her to my cousin because of the way she was going off on her, but I informed her that we speak on the phone every day and she knew everything that was going on in my life.

Additionally, one day my cousin and I were helping Paisley set up her new apartment when Nicole called and invited us to Matt party at his new place. The fact that she invited us made it clear that she had still been talking to him. She then proceeded to ask if I was going to go to Orlando with them two, my cousin was enraged and insisted that we go to the party. On the way there we were stopped by traffic and had to detour. It seemed liked everything was trying to stop us from going but we made it. Once we got to the party I was not feeling the vibe. Nicole had just arrived when I went to go get something out of the car and she spoke to me but I did not say too much to her. I knew what was about to happen when she went inside the party. It was obvious that she had been there before because she walked straight back to his room. That made me hot and bothered so I was doing petty things the whole time. I was having a conversation with one of the guest there and out of the side of my eye I saw that Nicole was getting ready to leave. My cousin also saw that and she got up so I followed. She asked her about the things she had written on twitter and then it went down from there. My cousin hit her first and I was trying to prevent them from fighting but Nicole would not let my cousin hair go so I popped her a couple of times so she could let go of her hair and actually fight her. The friend she was with was trying to jump in but Paisley politely moved her out the way. Once she let her go my cousin was ready to go again for round two but the guys at the party would not let her get to Nicole. All of a sudden, Matt came outside and yelled "come back inside the party, what are y'all fighting for?", I instantly started snapping. I tried to fight him a couple of times and was looking for a brick to bust the windows out of his car. He knew exactly what was going on and he was the caus of all it. I was so upset that I could not see what I was doing it felt like I went into a daze. My cousin had to body slam me on the ground so that I would calm down and they put me in the car to leave. After that I thought that the situation would be done but she kept going on snapchat saying she wanted to meet up and fight

my cousin again this time including me. I was furious and

anyone who knows me know I usually don't get physical with

people but I had enough including everything I was going

through, I was going to let her know not to mess with me

anymore. For some reason people felt that because I was

always involved in the church and usually let things roll off my

shoulders, they assumed that I could not and would not defend

myself. We drove to my old apartment complex University

Courtyard where she said to meet her, but she was not there.

Then she said to come over to her apartment complex which

was way on the other side of town, but I was so angry I went

anyway. As soon as we arrived she still wasn't there. She sent us

to the back of the complex and again she wasn't there so we

drove around to the front and when we noticed her car I

immediately told Paisley to stop and I hopped out. Nicole also

hopped out we began to fight. I knew I had no business fighting

because of my condition but that day I just had enough. I hit her

first and slipped to the ground. I remember thinking to myself that she was about to win the fight but once I got up it was on from there. I would not let her go until I felt like I was satisfied with how I handled her. For this reason, we fought four rounds. The very last round she thought it was a good idea to throw water in my face thinking that was going to stop me. Once she realized a bottle of water could not stop me she went to her car to get a bat. Every who was with me was furious. She knew that I had lupus and she wanted to fight and hit me with a steel bat. The bat still didn't make me stop defending myself every chance I got.

Once I was able to grab a hold of her on top of someone car, I punched her in the temple area three times with all of my might and I was done. We jumped in the car before anyone could call the police and went home. After the fight my hands could barely open, I was in so much pain from all the energy I put out to fight. The next day my neck was hurting and stiff from Nicole pulling on my hair during the entire fight.

# Chapter 6

## *"Train a child up in the way she should go; and when she is old, she will not depart from it"*

### *~Proverbs 22:6 KJV*

When things calmed down for me. I was reminded by the spirit of God that I allowed the devil to take control of the situation without praying about it and letting God handle it. I prayed so hard and was in church the following Sunday. I then realized I was searching for the same type of feeling I felt when I first fell in love with Stanley. I wanted more than dates, drama, and sex. I wanted to be with someone who visualized a future with me and who protect my heart at all cost. I cut off all tides with Nicole and Matt and started back focusing on school and my health. I felt free and single again. I was focusing more on God and continued to pray my way through everything.

My 22nd birthday was approaching and I was making plans, as to how I would celebrate. I wanted to make this one big, especially with all the drama that had been going on. Matt contacted me and wanted to talk, trying to justify his reason for making up such a big lie. I wasn't trying to hear anything that he had to say because I already made up in my mind that I was going forward and not looking back. When you go through a break up and really get over it, it's hard to allow anyone else to come in and take you through that pain again. My cousin Ruby who was involved in the fight with Nicole was living with me at the time. She wanted me to invite him to a birthday get together that I was going to throw at the last minute. I explained to her that I did not want him to be around and made a statement jokingly saying; if he came he knew that he had to bring me a gift. Matt and Ruby were messaging back and forth on snapchat and she told him to come. I told her that I did not want to talk to him because of what happened. At that point I was thinking of the right thing. If I decided to talk to him why I couldn't talk back to the mother of my God child, whose child I loved. She then began to say how can I speak back to Stanley and not talk to Matt. I told her that what Stanley and I had was something different than what I had with Matt. Stanley and I had history and no matter what he had done to me I still cared about his well-being, and it had nothing to do with wanting to be with him.

Although we had a bad break up, there were still moments when we really expressed our love for one another. Ruby then proceeded to head out the door to class. She had been living with me to get back on track with school and into a place to live. That day I called my older cousin Shardea to ask her opinion on the conversation Ruby and I had. Shardea, my uncle Willie's daughter is a very close cousin to me who is also like a sister. I was able to confide in her through everything and she always had my best interest at heart. She told me that she didn't think I was wrong for feeling how I felt about Matt coming to celebrate my birthday with me. I had her on speaker phone while I was trying to finish an assignment I needed to complete before I started my birthday weekend. During that time Ruby walked in the room doing what I called "half cleaning" the bathroom. After Shardea and I got off the phone

Ruby came in and asked me why did I make it seem to Shardea that she was serious about Matt coming over. I immediately looked at her confused and asked what she was talking about, she looked at me and said you heard what I said. I ignored her and called Shardea again to let her know what she just brought to my attention. We had already been on a different conversation and talking about something else and was taken aback that she would actually come in and assume that anyone was talking bad about her. The whole time I was on and off speaker phone with Shardea and if I was trying to hide something or "talk about" her I would not have had our conversation on speaker. When I went in the living room to talk to her she went ballistic, and started screaming and yelling. She said she didn't want to hear anything I had to say and if I was a real bitch I would have said something to her when she first asked me. I told her that I didn't know what she was talking about and she kept over talking me. I finally had enough of Ruby speaking to me as if she didn't have any respect for me or my house and this was not the first time. I expressed to her in a very enraged voice that we weren't even talking about her and Shardea was giving me her opinion as she always does.

Although I didn't have to explain that to Ruby I did anyway but that didn't change the situation it only escalated from there. She proceeded to get up all in my face, and because she was my cousin was the only reason why I didn't turn into a maniac on her. I called my grandma and told her that I had enough of her and her ways. Ruby made a comment that made me look at her different from that day forth. She stated that all I was going to do was get on the phone with my other side of the family and make it seem as if I'm so innocent. I was always taught to listen to what a person says when they are upset because that's when their true feelings show. I was hurt and disappointed that Ruby would take a phone conversation so far after all I had done to help her out. Ruby couldn't cook and didn't practice cleanliness while living with me. I didn't complain or judge her I just simply played my role as a supportive cousin and encouraged her to want to do better. Granted that people will do what they want, I saw much more potential in her than she probably seen herself.

She left and had my roommate take her to the bus station. During our argument, I told her to get the fuck out. I was so upset that she was treating me the way she was after everything I've done to help her. She knew that I would never let her go without food or a place to live, so her leaving was to prove a point, not that I was very serious about her leaving.

My birthday was coming within two days and I was not going to allow anyone to mess it up. I drove around my complex to calm down and make a phone call to who I realized in that very moment was my best friend Paisley. I explained to her what happened and she knew that I had enough. Paisley was always over my house so she was there to witness the disrespect and how Ruby would speak to me. She also thought that Ruby was over reacting. After my birthday, I was preparing to enjoy my spring break in Panama City Beach where all the spring breakers went from all over. Roxanne and Flo who was all a part of the click who were going. Jennifer and I met while working at the fast food restaurant Charley's freshman year. One day I asked her if she would take me home and she did. From that day forward Jennifer has always played a significant role in my life. Even though she had her own group of friends she always treated me the same. We didn't speak everyday but we spoke on the regular. Whenever I would cook she was always over or sometimes just to come to my house. She never came empty handed whether it was a bottle of wine or something for us to snack on. It was her last spring break in undergrad and we were going to celebrate, along with two other close friends of hers. We had the time of our lives and I had plenty of fun the couple of days we were there. I finally got to see what the hype was all about. As a freshman, I never really attended the frat parties or the house parties because I wasn't into that. Overall, it was a great time we spent together.

The spring break trip had come to an end. I had so much fun and was happy that I didn't have to spend a lot of money.

Once I arrived back down in Tallahassee I became so sick from drinking and not thinking of the consequences during a flare. I was more concerned about enjoying the last of my college days before they came to an end. Eventually I took myself to the doctor and was given medication for my symptoms. The doctor instructed me to take three prednisone tablets three times a day and then for me to reduce the dose 5mg every week.

Although I reached a point to where I didn't want to take any medication, I was taking the medicine because my grandma Doll was always hard on me about it. She always said, "I just want you to be better baby, so you can finish school". I told her not to worry that I would finish school and letting her down was not in my plans. From that day forth the spirit of God came over me again, and a voice in my head reminded me that I needed to find a church home. Considering being raised in church, I was always very skeptical and selective about joining just any church. I knew the ins and outs and how some church homes are not where God called you to be. I did what I knew how to do, which was pray for an answer. The following Sunday, I went to a church that I had been visiting with a few friends and I thought to myself it was finally time to join. When the pastor announced the call to the alter, there was a young man up there as well for prayer and to also become a member of the church.

They stated that they were praying because he had just lost his grandmother who raised him. I touched him in agreement that The Lord would cover him in his time of mourning. I knew exactly what he was going through because I was still going through it. Once we went to the back of the church we filled out papers and selected the type of work we wanted to do in the church. Then, I went home to do the usual, cooking Sunday dinner and preparing for my finals that were coming up because it was the last week of school and the end of the semester was approaching.

My mom called that Sunday to let me know that Grandma Doll was in the hospital but not to worry because she was going to be fine. I went on about my day and planned to come home that weekend to attend my big cousin Tara college graduation and planned to check up on her during the stay. I had a final every day that week up until Thursday.

# Chapter 7

*"In the year King Uzziah died, I saw the Lord*
*sitting upon a throne, high and lifted up;"*

*~Isaiah 6:1 NIV*

Early Tuesday morning I received a text from a distant cousin
saying; I'm so sorry baby, I'm praying for you" I was confused
because I had no clue what she was talking about. That's when I
figured out that someone had passed. I wasn't sure if it was my
grandmother Denise who has had me since I was born but it
wasn't.  My family didn't want to give me the news because
they didn't want me stressing about anything. I was in school
and finals were approaching so they thought that keeping the
news away from me would be in my best interest but in all
actuality, it made things worse for me. I didn't get a chance to
speak with her before she passed or even prepare myself for
what was about to happen. From my understanding. She had a
fall and that took her to the emergency room, she was running
short of breath after dropping my little sister off to school and

when she came home she had fallen. It was that day that I

realized God was starting to work in my life and show me the

signs I always prayed for. Isaiah was the first person I called

after not being able to get in contact with my friends. I told him

that my grandmother passed and I didn't know what I was going

to do. He answered me with the same statement in a confused

voice. I guess that was his way of reminding me that I was going

to be ok. He suggested I give him a call once I handled

everything in Miami with my family. When it was time to leave

Miami, I wanted to see him to talk about somethings I

discovered while being home for the funeral service but he

disappeared. I have reason to believe that I was thinking too far

into us at that moment so he backed away. I was always on

social media because I loved to keep up with the people I cared

about and I also enjoyed keeping up with tons of celebrities. I

held a special place in my heart for Isaiah so I was always on his

social media checking on him. I saw that he was traveling to

Tennessee and it instantly brought back memories from me

visiting my grandmother Doris-Ann every summer. The inside of his cabin house looked exactly how her house looked. I remember assuming that God was trying to show me that Isaiah was who I was assigned to be with.

Once we arrived I went over to my Doll baby house to be surrounded by family and friends. I sensed that from the confusion between my cousin Ruby and I, some members were acting very strange and stand-offish but I paid it no mind because at that point I had bigger things to worry about. I later went home and prepared myself for the funeral service. I traveled down the day before the home going so my roommate could do my hair. The next morning my mom and I had a make-up appointment. During the appointment, I was listening to Jazmine Sullivan whose album was just released a couple months before and trying to keep my mind off what was transpiring in my life at that very moment. My mother couldn't hold back the tears and she was beginning to mess up her make up. I will never forget that day. We wore white and I polished my nails purple like her favorite color. Which is something we shared. An older cousin asked if I wanted to be given an opportunity to speak on behalf of my great-grandmother and I didn't hesitate. Before figuring out what I was going to say, I prayed and asked the Lord to lead me. He told me to share my time with her but to also make it known to my grieving family that we needed to thank the lord not only for what he gives us but when he takes it away. My great grandma was the link in our family. If ever anyone was in a bind she was the go-to sister, aunt, cousin, etc. It tore me apart to see my great aunt so sad because she lost her best friend. I recall her asking my aunt Doris, who is a minister, for her help, because she had lost her sister. At that moment, I realized that not even my older aunt had not fully connected with the word of God. I felt an urgency to want to start speaking to her about what I knew Gods word said. She kept asking God why and instead I was thanking him for what he was about to do in our family. There were times when she would call me and tell me that she wasn't able to send me an allowance on time some months because how much she would help others out. My Doll baby was stern and loud but had a huge heart. She enjoyed eating, traveling, gambling and watching her nieces and nephews have a great time at family functions. After the funeral, we didn't go to her house for the repast because it was my God daughter 1st birthday party. There was an issue between my mom, granddad and uncle about giving me her car. I mentioned to my grandmother about a conversation grandma Doll and I were having about her car. She was telling me how she wasn't going to be able to drive her car soon, and when I asked her why her response was that she was getting old. I laughed and told her that she need to stop because she is not that old, she said yes I am, and I'm over weight and having heart problems. I told her well I'll take care of your car for you and she said to me "Michael bought me this car, I want you to have it but it would be up to him". Days before she passed the last conversation we had was discussing trying to get a job, getting on a particular Greek line that summer for Fall term, and trying to get my car fixed. She asked me if I was staying on my Dad's side of the family about getting a headstone placed down and why it wasn't done with all the funeral arrangements. Doll baby said to me that she didn't believe that they had done the right thing with my inheritance because nothing was making sense. I told her I would call my uncle again but no one was giving me a straight forward answer. At that time since my grandmother Doris-ann passed, my great grandmother and my maternal grandmother Denise were the only ones aiding me while I was away in college. For almost one year I was receiving disability assistance from the government. I received a letter a year later stating I needed to reapply and once I was available to finally reapply there was a very rude case worker behind the window.

She looked me up and down right before asking me why I waited until the last day. I didn't feel the need to have to explain to her that I was a college student and that was the only time I could come. I walked out of the building in disgust and was praying to God that I was blessed with a job I would be able to work. My car was not starting at the time so for a few months my roommate was allowing me to borrow her car for anything I needed to handle because she worked out of our apartment most days when she didn't have class. She was also able and willing to drive me to Miami for my great-grandmothers' funeral service. She was a very big help during this time of need and I will forever appreciate her for that.

After my great grandmother Doll passed, I was looking forward to starting a summer job while going to school. Before her passing we talked on the phone and I expressed to her how stressed out I was and how I did not want to have to ask her, and my grandma Denise for money all the time. Whenever I would ask my mom for money she would say she was going to send it once in a blue moon and it would not be much at all, or sometimes she would not send anything. While I was down for Doll baby service I took it upon myself to visit her grave site only to discover the headstone still was not placed down. Suddenly a voice in my head told me to go visit the church and this time not to let anyone know I was visiting. Once I arrived everyone was acting weird and very nervous. Usually, when I see them they are all over me and greeting me with open arms, but all of that stopped when I started asking questions about the headstone and inheritance. I was confused not only were my thoughts going wild but my anxiety had become uncontrollable.

First thing that came to mind was to go visit my dad to tell him what I had been feeling and how they showed themselves to me. He went to a file cabinet and pulled out a yellow envelope with the insurance papers that my grandmother had started for us on February 25th, 1992. The paper's showed the beneficiary as my dad then on another paper it displayed my uncle name who was the power of attorney over my grandmother estate. He listed his relationship as "SON" and as her not brother. There was also an older cousin involved with the changing of names because another policy showed the relationship as nephew but forgot to change the name from my uncle. I predicted that they were doing things so fast to try to hide what they've done but the few mistakes they made allowed God to show me exactly what they could have possibly done. The next day after visiting the church and speaking with my dad, I was heading back to T-town for an interview. I remember the day so clear. I was calling everyone on that side of the family that could have possibly known what they've done. Those that I suspected she was close to, I called because at that point I was in disbelief. I volunteered to drive the whole way back. Music and the ride home had become my therapy.

Tuesday morning, I woke up and got dressed for the interview. That night I couldn't sleep at all so I just ended staying up until it was time to get ready. Once I arrived the manager called me into her office and asked if I was ok to work. She noticed that something was wrong but I told her I was fine and still giving off the impression to people that I was fine. I was trying to keep myself occupied with school and work so that I could keep my grandmothers off my mind. We completed the interview and all I could remember is that I hoped she put me on the schedule. She said she would call the following week to begin training. I went in for training and it just so happened that my ex roommate sister was training the group of new hires. While she was explaining the job, what they expected, what they sell, and how to conduct ourselves on the phone she was giving an attitude. I wasn't the only one who noticed because once I asked a question and the way she responded made the other team member look at me with confusion. At that point I figured that she realized who I was and treated me different since then. There was a parking issue outside and she asked if anyone was in a silver Camry and I instantly thought of my grandmother but I drove my roommate car who had a white Honda. She said it needed to be moved but when no one claimed the car she nervously continued.

The questions she was asking I was sure to have my answers on point even the head manager that interviewed me was impressed. Once training was over, I went home to eat and dig more deeply into what I had discovered about my grandma Doris. The way the trainer was speaking to me had me thinking that she didn't put me on schedule because I sent them a

schedule of my classes so that I could choose my hours

accordingly. After days of waiting and dealing with all the

commotion that was going on, my mind had finally had enough.

# Chapter 8

*"If anyone will not welcome you or listen to your words, leave that home or town and shake the dust off your feet"*

*~Matt 10:14 NIV*

I went into a complete mental breakdown. I was on the medications heavily and did not know how much I was taking. Not knowing it was causing me to hallucinate. I was overdosing and didn't know it, in effort to not forget to miss taking them. The doctor instructed me to take 3 prednisone pills three times a day. At least, that's what I thought I heard. This caused confusion on top of the anger and disappointment I was feeling.

I was on Instagram looking at Isaiah pictures and still trying to put together this missing puzzle. Finally, I figured out what could have possibly happened with my grandmother's headstone and thought I completed life. I wanted to do everything in my power to get back at those who did her wrong. I called over Roxanne and Flo to explain to them what I discovered. I also told them about the back and forth that went

on about Doll baby car. Roxanne looked at me in confusion and

asked if I was talking about the grandma that bought my dress

for Nite Kap. I told her no, and I wasn't worried about that car

because I was more concerned about what my dad side of the

family had done to my grandma. At that point I realized that this

was something I was about to go through and only those

genuinely close to me would understand. I was talking to just

about everybody in my family that day. The only person who

noticed that something was wrong with me was my cousin

Shardea. She told my mom that I wasn't ok but she still didn't

budge, my grandmother called her and told her to see about me

and she didn't want to come. Her excuse was because she was

dealing with losing grandma Doll. I remember thinking I was

going to marry Isaiah. My thoughts were all over the place from

meds and I had the rest of my life planned. While the devil was

riding me, I noticed my roommate whose car I was using was

acting funny. My car was broken down for just about two

months and I was using her car to get to around. Paisley would come most times if her car was unavailable to take me to places such as grocery store or drug store. I was very firm about making sure to fill my roommate car up with gas or anything she needed because she was letting me borrow it. Once I came back from the nail shop under the impression that Isaiah was coming to Tallahassee to propose, I asked her a question and I noticed she had an attitude. I didn't understand why she was acting so funny out of nowhere. I was already feeling some type of way about my other friends treating me different and now her. Roxanne and Flo had just received their cars two months before and for them to have been close to me no one made sure I was ok or had a ride to anywhere I needed to go. I had to ask. I figured that they made their decision to side with my cousin Ruby about the altercation that had taken place. So, between Paisley's sister car, Jennifer and my roommate car, that was my only reliable transportation. During this time, I was frustrated because I wanted to have my own and I felt as if I was being let down by those I have always been there for. When Roxanne and Flo left my apartment the night I called and asked them to come over so I could speak with them about what had been going on, the everyday phone calls stopped. At that point I felt as if everyone was against me. I started noticing my friends speaking to someone who didn't like me, and hanging around the very same people they spoke ill of. Not taking the medication correctly didn't help my thoughts at all. It was like I had just stepped into a movie. The medicine had me thinking that the sorority I was trying to become a member of had others communicating with old friends and they were telling them not to choose me for the line. Additionally, there were some maintenance issues arousing in my apartment and the office was taking forever to act on it. I discovered that an ex-friend of mine name Tory was working with student housing along with another girl who wasn't so fond of me. I figured that the work orders I had been putting in were being deleted by either of the two. Instantly, I jumped in my roommates' car and drove over to the complex they both supposedly worked at. Once I arrived they were not there. There was a boy who was working the front desk and with fear in his eyes he said there was no manager available to speak with me. That day I was running around literally like a chicken with its head cut off.

Since the day I discovered that my grandma Doll had passed and what my dad side of the family had done, I did not sleep. I was hurt, angry, and full of rage. I called a cousin who is like an aunt, to tell her about what I discovered she immediately said that I was the devil and for me to stay away from "her" family as if I wasn't a part of it. My natural reflex led me to exchange nasty words to her over the phone and she began to tell me that I was the reason my great-grandmother Albertha was in the hospital. Once I hung the phone up with her I called my dad and asked if my great-grandmother was ok and he said she was just fine and sitting home. They kept her out of the circle so that she wouldn't give them an opinion. The next day I was still enraged and full of anger ready to fight anyone who I thought had bad intentions. That day my roommate Kandice started getting slick about me using her car, I would talk to her and she would walk by and not say anything. I was trying to figure out why she was treating me that way. I went in her room ready to fight with a pot in my head. My reason for the pot was because I remembered when I was fighting Nicole I had no strength because my lupus was flared up. So, to ensure that she wouldn't take me down, the pot was the only way I felt like I could protect myself. She threatened to call the police on me and I called my mom immediately on the phone to let her know what had transpired. Apparently, her mom had called my mom telling her that she was going to press charges on me if they didn't get me from around her. I remember my family calling my older cousin and girlfriend to come get me and take me to their house. I didn't want to go because I thought that Isaiah wasn't going to be able to find me once he "came in town". I thought to myself that everyone was trying to keep me from being happy and now that they've discovered I could possibly have a pretty penny they wanted to be around. My mom sent her friend to pick me up from his house. Before I went to their house my mom friend close cousin called and asked was I ok. I told her that I was ok, I was just angry and in total disbelief that all of this was happening to me at one time. Once I was picked up from the home it felt as if I was riding around in the car for hours. We were all the way on the other side of Tallahassee that I had not seen before so I had become very suspicious on top of the medication having an impact on altering my thoughts. Those thoughts lead me to believe that my dad was becoming President and the world was about to change for the better and all God needed me to do was figure out what "they" had done. Every day since the day I found out about my family selfish acts, I had been speaking with my dad if not twice, three times a day. Of course, my mom and others believed that my dad was putting thoughts in my head about everything and not paying attention to the possible side effects from the medication I was on. Specially growing up without having my father in my life. Since I was about 6, his family lead me to believe that my dad didn't believe in God. For years, I believed them simply because of the way my dad dress. He wore wraps and when I asked why they told me he thought he was the "Messiah". I was always sad and depressed whenever an event came up that recognized fathers' because all I could talk about is the first six years of my life. The next stop with my mom friend was at a Walmart out of the city of Tallahassee. We drove from there to I-10 and eventually ended up in at her cousin house was also a friend of my mom. She was also acting afraid and weird, and she did not want me coming into her home. I figured that they were also involved in all that had been going on and I was ready to fight them. They kept asking me if I wanted to go home and I said no because I was thinking of the job and still thinking Isaiah was coming to get me, to make me his wife. The cousin asked if I was angry and I told her no, that I was ready to go and that I just didn't feel good. I wasn't eating and getting absolutely no sleep. She said that she would take me to the doctor so that I can get treatment from them but instead we arrived at a center in Tallahassee I was unfamiliar with. When asked where we were she told me that there were counselors inside who would talk to me and try to help me with the way I was feeling because I was dealing with a lot. I didn't believe her so I hesitated but eventually they took me inside to sit in the waiting area. Once I stepped foot inside I realized at that moment where I was. After

waiting 30 mins in the lobby area, the doctor called me in and

started to examine me. He asked who brought me to the

facility, what was going on, and how I was feeling. From the

conversation I had with the doctor I figured they were going to

let me go home. Next, they had a nurse come escort me to a

room with double beds. There was a woman laying down in

there and I remember becoming so frightened to sleep in a

room with someone they considered mentally ill because I was

not mentally ill. I ended up trying to fight the staff in the facility

so that I could be released. Instead they gave me an injection

on my side. The next day early that morning I found myself

waking up with blurry vision signing papers to be admitted into

the mental hospital. Once I went into a room and woke up in

time for lunch that I did not eat. I went outside to a gated area.

A woman that was also there told me that I was going home

that day and my husband was waiting on me because he

wanted to propose to me. I figured that I was not crazy and I

knew what I was talking about the whole time. Once we went

back into the room the doctors called me in to evaluate me to be discharged. He then brought my mom and aunt in to listen to me. Once I was released they took me to my apartment, I packed my clothes, and we went back over to her friend's cousin house Ms. Angela.

We spent the night and they planned to head to Miami the next morning. Eventually, I ended up waking up in the middle of the night thinking they were going to try to take me away from Isaiah. My mom threatened that she would take me back to "that place" if I didn't stop being rebellious and I told her to take me because I refused to leave Tallahassee. Once I realized we were on the way to Miami I went insane. I remember telling my mom how she was dating the pastor at her church and that I knew all about it.

# Chapter 9

## *"Be not afraid nor dismayed by reason of this great multitude; for the battle is not yours but Gods'"*

### *~II Chronicles 20:15 KJV*

We argued all the way to Miami because she kept asking me what I was talking about. I told her that she knew exactly what I was talking about and that was why I wasn't able to be chosen on the sorority line I was interested in. I believed because the girls were putting in word that my mom was messing around with a pastor. I began to think that anything I ever said about God and having a relationship with him no one would believe me because of my mother's actions. My mother took it upon herself to take me to another mental behavior center once we reached Miami near Jackson Hospital. I called her a liar and told her that I knew about everything and was stating everything I knew. I reminded her that the pastor cousin was someone who had been spending the night with us whenever he came down from Atlanta to visit or make his doctor appointments. He was a very nice guy I treated him with respect and held conversations here and there. He had diabetes and was losing sight in his eyes, so he couldn't see that well in light areas. He also had a wife who he lived with but was talking to one of my mom friends who she met through him. I figured they became close because her and the "other women" had similar situations going on. However, my mom had a hard time getting me out of the car to go inside to be evaluated again. Once I went inside of what she told me was a hospital she started arguing with me again. She made me believe that they were going to give me fluids and sedate me but that was not the case. I was raising my voice in rage because of what I knew was about to happen. She convinced a guy working there that I was mentally ill. She told them that my dad was in a cult and somehow, he had influenced my mind and have me acting crazy. The guy that was working the front desk escorted me to speak with the psychiatrist so that he would be able to evaluate me. Once the doctor and I were in the same room alone I explained to him all that had been going on he said that it seemed to him as if

nothing was wrong. However, the guy at the front and my mom

insisted that I be admitted. Next thing I remember is singing and

crying out to God to take me away from this situation because I

was being misunderstood. They placed me in a room and told

me to take off my clothes and jewelry. After given a gown they

took me upstairs to give me a room. Once I realized this was

happening I started singing again. The nurse working the station

was telling me to shut up because I may wake up the others,

she also told me that my singing was horrible and I needed to

be quiet. I politely ignored her and did not go to the bed they

eventually assigned me to. There were papers they wanted me

to sign and I refused. I thought to myself that I was not going to

sign any paper that would keep me in that facility. Staff workers

became suspicious as well. I thought that there were two

people who knew of my dad side of the family and assumed

they were informed so that's why they treated me poorly. This

was the worse experience of my life. I stayed there for three

weeks, one week right after Grandma Doll passed. One day I

was asking the doctor when I was going home and every time I asked he ignored me. I took it upon myself to knock on the office door to speak with him about releasing me. Once I knocked and the door was open, I asked when did he think they were going to release me and he began to attempt to slam the door in my face. The door almost closed on my foot and my natural instinct was to hit him. Out of nowhere a woman who was a staff member, and also someone I suspected knew of my dad family started hitting me while another staff was holding me. From that point on I was forcefully held down and given an injection. For 30 minutes, I was fighting the medication and not allowing it to knock me out but eventually I went to sleep. Still under the medication I was woken up by the same staff member who was holding me down allowing his co-worker to attack me, came in and served me dinner. I remember this day clearly because dinner that night was spaghetti. I never ate the food that they served us because it was gross and the facility was unsanitary. They forced me to eat the food by forcing the spoon in my mouth, while allowing it to fall onto the gown they provided me to wear. By this time, I was nauseous and ended up vomiting the entire meal. Every day I waited for one of my family members to bring me food. Most days it was my mom, but I knew it was only because she was feeling guilty about having me admitted. Noon time was the time they allowed the patients to go outside in a closed-in area, being closely watched for fresh air. There was one woman who I sat next to at one of the picnics table and she started talking to me. At first, I didn't know if I should hold a conversation with her because I didn't know if she was mentally ill but she proceeded to tell me that she loved my voice and she will be praying for me. She said, I should also take some time to write about whatever I was going through, she made Dolls and she said the next Doll she made she was going to name it "Danielle". I had become very close with a woman who was admitted in the facility as well. Her name was Miranda she was a little off but for the most part she was in her right mind. We began talking because she made a statement that made me laugh. Miranda had my back the entire time I was there. She didn't let anyone harm me or mistreat me, and when they were about to give a shot she would start acting crazy. If the staff was giving me a hard time she would make ways for them to treat me correctly. One time she realized what my mom was doing to me. She was about to fight my aunt that my mom sent to bring me food. I remember her saying that she didn't like that and once they placed her in an isolated room she shouted through the glass saying "don't do her like that "while crying at the same time. I will never forget Miranda, because the moment I met her I was no longer afraid of anyone in there.

After all the "Doll" talk I was feeling a little down and trying to figure out what she meant by telling me to write about it. Once we came back inside after 30 mins of fresh air she went to her side of the building and I went to my assigned side. Later that evening it was visiting time. My older cousin Shardea walked in with journal that read "Believe you can and your already there" and it was that moment that I realized the Lord wanted me to share my story. I was going through so much mental illness and physical illness at the time and it seemed as if I was the only person who knew what was happening in my life. Whenever, I would begin to speak about the signs, I figured God was trying to show me, everyone else thought I was crazy. I became silent and did in my heart what I felt God need me to do. I didn't know where to start or even where to end, I just knew God had given me the vision and it was my duty to do his will. I decided that I was going to use every negative detail in my life and turn it into a stepping stone to my purpose. My purpose was to tell my story, how good God has been to me, and that he is truly real. I realized that I didn't have to be perfect to be a warrior of God, and my mistakes or even the place I was in my life did not detour me from keeping my relationship with God.

*"No eye has seen, no ear has heard, and no mind has imagined what God has prepared for those who love him"*

*~I Corinthians 2:9 NIV*

*"Jesus said unto him, if thou canst believe, all things are possible to him that believeth"*

*~Mark 9:23 KJV*

A couple of days later, my mom came in along with one of her best friends' aunt. They sat down to give me food my mom cooked and ask questions. The staff were asking if she would like for me to go home because I was back to routinely taking my meds and was doing much better. She began to talk to me and asked if I still thought she was having an affair with the pastor at the church she attended. With extreme hesitation I answered yes, she said to the aunt; "See, she's still not right". I then changed my answer and said no I didn't think that she was messing around with the pastor and it was just my mind so that I would able to leave. I was so hurt because she still didn't convince the staff or doctors to let me go home and left me in there for another night. I had no insurance so my stay was going to be billed on my credit to cover the time I was there. The next day, the new doctor who was assigned to me said that I was fine and she didn't see why I was still there but the doctor who I got into the altercation with insisted I have an MRI done before being released. The results from the MRI came back and showed that everything was normal. After two more days I was released and before leaving I had to get the prescription for my medications I needed to take daily. I refused to take the medication the were prescribed to me for psychiatric reasons but my mom insisted and waited until it was ready. The wait for the medication was pointless because once we got home I did not take it. She took me to a restaurant called finger licking in the area, did a couple of drop offs to sell some weight loss pills and we went home.

# Chapter 10

## *"Be on guard. Stand firm in faith. Be courageous. Be strong"*

### *~I Corinthians 16:13 NIV*

My little sister was with her Dad who was also like a dad to me. His name was Ralph. Ralph was such a great father figure to me and before Raven was born I was considered his only daughter. His son from a previous relationship and I were close so I affectionally called him my little brother. We traveled almost all the time, between Universal Studios or Island of Adventure we experienced those theme parks more than once. One weekend we planned to leave town and he and my mom had gotten into an argument. She didn't want to go anymore and she didn't want me to go either. She decided to go missing on him and not answer his phone calls so he called my grandmother and asked her to get me ready because he was on his way to pick me up. My grandmother also considered Ralph as a son and loved him as such so she didn't second guess about sending me off with him. He told her that she didn't need to pack me any clothes because he would buy me some once we got there.

Immediately once we arrived, we went to the Nike store in the outlet and he told me to pick up whatever I wanted. Nick and I always matched on these trips from head to toe. If he had a head band I also had one. The room was set up as a double suite and we were right next to Ralph. One night I walked into the room where he was and saw a naked girl, I went back in mine and Zee's room. I was scared because I thought I was about to get in trouble but it was blown off. I think he was more scared would I tell my mom when we got back. That morning his friends and their girlfriends all came along to have lunch and we rode mini hummers around town. After that I rode on the back of his friend Wilson's mini hummer, he was riding very wild and we almost flipped over. Ralph blasted him so badly to the point where he told him he would hurt him about his daughter. I ended up getting in his car. Ralph showed his love and protected me like a father and it really showed that day. Although I was scared for my life in that very moment it was one of the most fun times I've experienced. Two weeks after

being discharged from Jackson Memorial, I was headed to a

concert and got word that he had passed suddenly without

warning. With all that I had just endured, I knew that my body

could not take any more loss. For that reason, I could not attend

his funeral services to say my final goodbyes.

Now that I was home and my mother had finally given

my phone back that she snatched from me during the

commotion, I saw all those that had been calling. I was also

trying to figure out how I was going to withdraw from the

courses I enrolled in for that summer term and was due to

attend. My aunt Judy was helping to assist me with that, so she

emailed my dean and my advisor. Once I settled in, I texted

Roxanne back from when she text. When I responded, she

called right away. She asked if I was ok and she had been trying

to get in contact with me and no one was giving her any

information. I began to explain to her what went down and I felt

that she and Flo were not being very good friends because I

noticed how they both sided with my cousin Ruby when we got into our huge argument. My mother overheard my conversation on the phone and starting yelling, and cursing telling me to get off the phone. I told Roxanne I would call her back once I got a chance to talk and hung up. I asked my mom why was she yelling like that and why did she say what she said so loud while I was on the phone with her. She said I didn't need to be stressing about that situation and I explained to her that I wasn't stressing I was just explain to her what I had been going through and how I was feeling.

I went back to Tallahassee to finish out my lease and get my classes handled and figure out the next step. It was stressful because not only did I need to worry about moving my stuff but my cousin Ruby stuff that she left when she called herself leaving Tallahassee. I told her that I could not move any of her stuff out because I already didn't have that much help moving mine. She said she would be there to move her things before the 31st and she ignored my text. The day I moved out was a week early because I had things to take care of and I was informing her she needed to get it before then. When the 31$^{st}$ came she had Flo to call me to see if her laptop was there and I told that I already informed her that I placed all her things in the hallway closet. Also, I asked was the laptop the only thing she was worried about? Mostly, Ruby's clothes were there including shoes. Moreover, I was having a hard time trying to inform the school about what I had gone through so they would be able to take the charges off my account for those courses I was scheduled to take that summer.

Once I met with the advisor of Occupational Therapy I then learned that I was falling into the excess credit bracket and soon I would have to come out of my pocket for my classes that I needed, as if I was not already experiencing life trials. She suggested that I change over my major to Interdisciplinary Studies, to graduate without coming into the problem of excess credits and not be able to afford classes. With this, I would still be able to take the courses towards Pre-Occupational Therapy with a concentration in health and a minor in Biology. I was very sad to hear this news that I was being held back because of my grades that were falling due to my illness and not able to perform to the best of my ability. Also, it meant that I had to sit out another summer because of my illness which would push me back even more and I was expecting to graduate December of 2015 or Spring 2016. I was also moving and now needed to find some where to live alone because I decided that it was best to live alone, once my roommate Katia and I got into it. Once I moved out I stayed between Paisley sister house or my mom friend cousin house.

This time staying at her house was very different, instead of a guest I felt like a burden and I didn't feel very comfortable. I was so happy when I was finally able to find an apartment but this time I needed my dad to be my guarantor because grandma Doll was no longer alive and I didn't have any of her information. The rent for this apartment in my opinion, was very high but it was my last resort because everything that was furnished and affordable was taken. My grandmother and mother agreed to go half on my rent until I could pay it up with my financial aid refund check. Of course, my grandmother was the only one keeping up her share of the deal and almost always sending me extra to cover groceries, toiletries, and medication I needed. My mother never seemed to understand that I had needs besides the rent she barely helped pay. Grandma Denise was working, so whenever I would run into a problem with my rent or any other bills she was always there picking up the slack. I wasn't the type to go out and shop buying unnecessary things without taking care of my responsibilities first, so my grandmother never mind giving me money when it came down to helping provide for me. She sent my friends money as well just to show appreciation to them for helping me out on the many days I couldn't help myself. Every month that it was time to pay my rent my mother had an issue. She could never pay my rent on time. One day my grandmother became so upset that she told her about herself. From then on, she told my grandma that she will no longer be helping pay my rent and that she would handle it until I was doing better and able to work. For one month, she paid the rent on time and after that it was problems ever since. I was so stressed out and overwhelmed with all that was happening I noticed my skin started changing. My face began to break out in dark spots. The breakout started on my eye lids first by forming pealing sores. This is when I realized I could get my eyebrows waxed anymore because my skin was so sensitive. My hands were forming hard blisters that would itch if they my hands wasn't moisturized. Honestly, I felt like a creature. I thought to myself that I was never going to finish school because I felt myself going into shut down mode and I would not perform well on test and assignments. At first, I paid it no mind and figured it would clear up but instead it got worse. Once my friends started changing toward me, I thought that it didn't bother me as much but my skin was showing otherwise. Every year as a group we told each other our birthday plans. Flo birthday was approaching and she decided to have a party and she text me in a group message with 20 plus people included. I took that as if she didn't really want to invite me but if I want to come I can come. On top of that she invited my cousin Ruby. However, Jennifer and Paisley went. Paisley said she wanted one of them to ask where I was but they didn't. A few weeks later Flo text Paisley and told her that she didn't like the distance between them and Paisley expressed to her that she didn't like the way I was treated. She mentioned that she didn't like how they invited me for drinks one day and no one responded to me when I asked what time, but on snapchat everyone was out having drinks. Flo then began to tell Paisley that she didn't know what I was telling her and Paisley said it wasn't anything I was telling her it was what she saw. The same night we ended up seeing Flo, along with Roxanne and Samantha. Flo made eye contact with me but walked straight passed me. Samantha saw me and spoke which prompted Roxanne to also speak to me. She said; "Hey Danielle" in a very malicious manner so I ignored her and continue talking to my friend who sat in front of me. Once Paisley recognized that they walked passed her after she had just finished having a conversation with her through text. Prior to them walking in the restaurant my cousin Ruby texted Paisley and said that they

needed to talk and it was a bunch of flaw shit going on that she

didn't like. Paisley immediately asked her what she was talking

about and when she responded Paisley waited until she was off

work to have time to deal with that situation. I don't recall what

happened on the phone with Ruby and Paisley but I do

remember it ending cool on their end. One day my Paisley sister

needed to use a big curling iron and I remembered that Flo still

had it at her house and once she asked her for them, a few days

later Tianna texts Paisley about situation they already had

figured out. So, because Flo was asked for the curlers back I

guess Ruby felt the need to want to start some shit. With all

that was happening I was under a lot of pressure. I began to

develop sores on the bottom of my feet on top of the sores on

my face. That prevented me from walking long distance, also on

my hands which made it hard writing and driving. But I drove

myself to class every day. The sores were so bad that my ears

and fingers would bleed. I tried all the options to get better. I

even tried to go to counseling to get help to cope with all that

I've been through and the changes my body was experiencing. Everything had become too much to handle and I had become over whelmed. The main thing I was trying to remind myself to do was remain calm and focused. That spring semester I failed one class. The class was in the evening and parking was so hard to find, meaning most times I had to walk a distance to class. As stated before, my feet and hands were very sore and tender. If someone was to scratch me accidently I would begin to bleed. I could never focus in class from the pain I was experiencing and it resulted in poor test scores. We were in the second week of April and I planned to take pictures to promote the book. I was very grateful for the support I received from my older cousin who is a photographer who did everything for free. She traveled from Jacksonville to Tallahassee to take photos and help bring my vision to light. Earlier that month I spoke with my mother about sending me 50 dollars so that I can get my hair washed and treated, and she said she would be able to send it. I was using the little money I saved to purchase the items I needed for the photoshoot. Of course, when it was time for me to get my hair washed for the photoshoot she said she didn't have the money and she wasn't going to send it when she did get it, because she didn't want to support a book that she assumed I would be bashing her in. From that moment forward I realized that my mother was not someone that I could count on. I started to revisit the thoughts of her placing me in the mental behavior center realizing the whole time I was in there was mainly because I was acknowledging that I knew about her and the pastor's affair. There was a certain point in time where I was thinking that what she was saying was true and that I my thoughts were misconstrued based off assumptions. However, in that moment God revealed to me everything I needed to know about her. I've always longed for a close relationship with my mother. When I met my best friend Paisley and her mother it made me want the relationship even more. I figured that if Paisley whose mother and father were on drugs and in the streets, could develop a relationship with her and her siblings, then it would do me no harm to work on my relationship with mine. I came home again after that spring semester of 2016 ended. My mom is always being a negative Nasty and always choosing to speak with disrespect towards me. Even if I was calling her for something simple she sounded aggravated. It was damaging in a sense, to always ask my grandmothers for everything and the few times I went to my mom for anything, I was rejected and treated as if I was a nuisance. When it came to things I needed my mom was absent. I wanted her to understand that it wasn't about money or clothes but just simply being there to support me 100 percent. It seemed as if I was going to never get better and she blamed me for my sickness. We ended up getting into an argument that consequently resulted in a physical altercation. Once that happened she called the police and she had them take me to CHI mental behavioral center.

There I was evaluated and started saying the same thing I was saying when I spent those three weeks a year prior in Jackson Memorial Hospital. I informed the nurse at the station that absolutely nothing was wrong with me and my mom was just upset because she never wanted to hear the truth. She had

been lying to me and making me believe that it was something

wrong with me. The officers told them that I was being Baker

Act by my mother. I thought that I was only going to stay for

one day but it ended up being a whole week. This time for the

third time I was in a mental behavioral center for Memorial Day

weekend. My grandmother Denise during this time was out

working in Iowa for just a little over a year now but she was

down this time. Every day she was bringing me food and

hygiene products. I also began to believe that Isaiah and I still

had a chance, and I wasn't thinking out of order. Eventually I

realized I thought too far into the "situation". Other than that,

everything I was saying a year prior when I was placed in the

crisis center in Tallahassee and in Miami at Jackson was true.

The incident that led everyone to believe I needed to be put in a

mental crisis center instead of taking me to the hospital like

they convinced me they would, was between my roommate

Katia the night after coming at her with a pot. I thought to

myself since she was acting funny now with letting me borrow her car to go to places simply as the nail salon up the street or the grocery store around the corner I figured that she was involved with Flo, Roxanne, and Ruby.

After the incident there was whole I put in her bathroom wall the day of our altercation. I told her to find out how much it would be to get it fixed and I would give her the money once I received my financial aid from school. She was upset all together so she wanted me to act at that very moment and I honestly couldn't do anything about it. Some of her friends were over that day as well, and they were really confused about what was going on with me. I started telling them my whole life story and why I suspected Katia was involved with the girls I was no longer cool with. Eventually, Katia and I stopped talking after the altercation and I always prayed she would understand what I was going through one day when things cooled down.

# Chapter 11

*"Who can find a virtuous woman?  For her price is far above rubies."*

*~Proverbs 31:10 KJV*

My grandmother drove back with me back up to school and stayed for a week. The time she was there lifted a big weight off my shoulders. She cooked and helped me clean. Of course, I could do all those things for myself but going to school and trying to keep up with cleaning became tiring, so I appreciated her coming there to be a help. My feet were still healing so I couldn't drive how I wanted plus I had to put cream on my hands twice a day. While I was taking my summer courses she drove me to and from class. One Wednesday we went to bible study at her best friends' sister and husband church. The church was in a small building not too far from campus. This was my first time ever attending this church. We enjoyed the topic and was getting ready to let out. The pastors' wife, who was my grandmothers best friend sister, stopped the pastor before the dismissal prayer. She said that God was telling her not to leave with speaking to somebody. She said; "white hat" I paid it no mind because there was a woman sitting in the same row as I also with a white hat. The woman stood up and she said; "no not you, you young lady". In total shock I answered and said "yes?", with a look of confusion. She spoke about everything that I was feeling and had been going through. The lord wanted her to remind me that he was listening to me and he needed me to trust him more than I already did. Additionally, she spoke about how there were a lot of enemies against and most are some people I don't even know are against me. She said they tried to attack my mind and make it seem as if I was crazy. Next, she mentioned my grandmothers and how I have never been the same from when I lost Grandma Doris, and losing Grandma

Doll set me off completely. She said you know what your paternal grandmother brothers and sisters done to you and they know that you know, but they were trying to make you believe that you had no idea. You have been so confused in the thoughts and your mind has been running completely wild. She mentioned my lack of sleep and how I was up all night trying to figure out what was missing. The lord told her from family to friends God is getting ready to reveal and he wants my heart and mind to be strong when he did, so I needed to trust him. She also said that it was something I needed to remember that my grandmother told me at my aunt's house the last time I saw her and in order for me to remember, God wanted me to get my mind and thoughts in order. Before this night at bible study I was trying figure things out on my own and fight my battles alone without letting him take total control. I became humble and began to work on trusting God more than ever.

*"Humble yourselves in the sight of the Lord, and he shall lift you up."*

*~ Matt 4:10 KJV*

131

Through all the things I have been through the most important thing I've learned is to trust God. I was feeling rejected by the people that I love the most and starting to believe there was not a God. I mean I had every right to feel that way because these are people that I've been around since I was a little girl. Overall, I found comfort in his word. The world will have you depressed and angry, but if we focus on who is in control of the whole world, it would be a better place. After going through some of my favorite uplifting scriptures and stories in the Bible I realized God mains focus was to spread love. I no longer wanted revenge against no one.

*"Dearly beloved, avenge not yourselves, but rather give place to wrath; for it is written, Vengeance of Mine, I will repay".*

*~ Romans 12:19 KJV*

I realized in this moment that what I could do was not compared to how God can handle the situation and people who've hurt me. I was preparing to graduate in the upcoming Fall semester and things were beginning to unfold. Still not resting as I should, but I finally remember what my grandmother told me. She crawled to the guest room at my aunt house and failed to wake me up from my sleep to talk long enough before my aunt came. She said with fear in her eyes after hearing my aunt come towards us "Dannie, I didn't get to sell that house" I didn't know how to receive it and every thought in my mind became cloudy since that day. This is one thing I know for sure.

> **"Bless them that curse you, and pray for them which despitefully use you."**
>
> **~ Luke 6:28 KJV**

I love my family very dearly and I'm the happiest times when we are all together having a great time. Some have truly hurt me and I have forgiven them all but I am still hurt. I could have never imagined that most of them sadly will not be a part of many milestones in my life. I've learned to love myself when it came down to relationships because I could not love anyone else if I did not love myself. I became celibate and praying for God to send me my husband on his time. So, I'm thankful for the pain and hurt I had to go through in order, for God to use me and for that I'm forever grateful. The purpose of this book was to inform you all that the Lord is truly real and when we cast everything on him, he will supply all of our needs. There were plenty of nights and days when I knew it was nobody but God that brought me through. Those I expected to be there for me and have my back didn't but in the end God was the only one. He placed great people around me and until I started releasing those who weren't for me he started blessing me. I was losing sight of God and his word and depending on people for happiness other than God. It is true that he gives each of us a gift, and once we solely focus on him, he will help us find it. My main goal today and for the rest of the years God has granted me here on this earth is to spread love, will and forgiveness. I hope this book has inspired and come into touch with many of you, not only to become more aware of Lupus but to also have a different outlook on developing a closer relationship with God. Nonetheless, I leave you with these words,

*"But blessed is the one who trust in the lord, whose confidence is in him"*

*~Jeramiah 17:7 NIV*

*Special Thanks..*

*"So in everything, do to others what you would have them do to you"*

*~Matt 7:20 NIV*

*I want to give honor to my lord and savior Jesus Christ, my family and friends that have supported and continue to pray for me. I also want to thank:*

- *Sabrina Samoan Photography*
  *Sabrinasamoan.com*
  *904-274-1977*

- *First Class Faces*
  *Takema Russ*
  *786-757-9052*

- *Editor*

*Shardea Bowens-Matthews*

*For unknowingly providing me with the tool that started this journey.*

64691076R00077

Made in the USA
Middletown, DE
18 February 2018